Temiskaming Treasure Trails,
the earliest years

Peter Fancy

Published by
Highway Book Shop
Cobalt, Ontario. P0J 1C0

Copyright © 1992 by
Peter Fancy
ISBN 0-88954-358-5

Canadian Cataloguing in Publication Data

Fancy, Peter, 1932-
    Temiskaming treasure trails

Includes bibliographical references and index.
Partial contents: v. 1. The earliest years.
ISBN 0-88954-358-5 (v. 1)

1. Fort Témiscaming (Ville-Marie, Quebec) -
History. 2. Témiscamingue (Quebec : Census
division) - History.   3. Fur trade - Quebec
(Province) - Témiscamingue (Census division) -
History. 1. Title.

FC2945.T6F36 1992   971.4'13   C92-094293-8
F1054.T6F36 1992

CONTENTS

ILLUSTRATIONS

ACKNOWLEDGMENTS

Out of the Hudson's Bay Company archives and her related researches, Elaine Mitchell's *Fort Timiskaming and the Fur Trade* emerged as a richly detailed description of early Temiskaming times. Her numerous articles in the Company's *Beaver* magazine expanded certain stories. With similar affection for his subject, Augustin Chenier's *Notes Historiques sur le Témiscamingue* remembered particular traders, missionaries and lumbermen leading the settlement way to Lake Temiskaming. The faithful energy of these writers revealed a cast of characters whose stubborn explorations north made adventurous sense of Chevalier de Troyes' earliest seventeenth century spirit.

During the 1954 and 1956 summers, Paul Sweetman assisted Frank Ridley's Ontario archaeological excavation of a mainland site on Bonin's Farm north of the Montreal River. Washed away by a Hydro dam, the site is gone today, but here in the top levels of the excavation they found parts of guns, gun flints and lead musket balls along with rusted knife blades. This evidence, Paul Sweetman says, is strong enough to suggest that the eighteenth century fur traders from Montreal could have established a post here, between the times when they left the wave-eroded shores of Meadow Island and built the fort farther north at Obadjiwanan Narrows. This present *Temiskaming Treasure Trails* story, however, knowingly compresses the intervening period.

FOREWORD

Aleck Paul, the second chief of the Temagami band of Ojibwa, once remembered the story of:

a boy who used to set his snares for his living. One day he saw a track where the snow was melted, and after a while he decided to set his snares there and catch the animal that made the tracks. So he set his snare and went away. That track was the sun's track and when the sun came by next day, it got caught. The sun didn't rise the next day and there was steady darkness. The people began to be puzzled. 'Where did you set your snare?' they asked him. He told them, and they went to look. There they saw the sun caught, but no one could go near enough to loosen it. A number of animals tried to do this, but they all got burned. At last the Beaver-Mouse managed to cut it with his teeth and freed it. But, his teeth got burned with the heat, and so they are brown to this day, but the sun is here and we have the daylight. (Speck, Memoir 71)

Measureless winds and suns chipped volcanic peaks down into ocean depths, and glaciers shaved earthquake folds flat. Then after water filled the rift valley of Lake Temiskaming, creature life crept on to the land. And later people came. Wandering through thick forests, they hunted wild game for food, clothes and shelter. Yet sometimes, spoiled by plenty, they starved under winter's heavy ice, leaving only a few survivors to sing of summer. Held close by families, though, the tribe grew strong in this home of sky, earth and trees.

In 1534, Jacques Cartier sailed up the St. Lawrence River in search of China, but revealed instead a lush wealth of Canadian furs. So Champlain, sixty-nine years later, with monopoly fur trade in mind, settled a Canadian colony at Quebec. Yet jealous Dutch and English traders would agitate the Iroquois to scalp the French and their Huron friends. New France shrieked treason when Radisson and Groseilliers persuaded London, England, merchants to start the Company of Adventurers of England Trading into Hudson's Bay. And then began the story of *Temiskaming Treasure Trails.*

Fur traders from Montreal soon created the Compagnie du Nord to send their own ships into Hudson Bay and build posts in competition with the English. South of the Bay, on Lake Temiskaming, the French built another fortified post from which they could intercept Indian winter fur catches on their way to the English. Countering armed resistance the Compagnie du Nord, in 1686, hired Chevalier de Troyes to lead a successful attack up the

Ottawa River-Lake Temiskaming route against the rival posts on Hudson Bay. Two years later, in vengeful turn the Iroquois destroyed Fort Temiskaming.

Though abandoned for thirty years, French fur trade resumed on Lake Temiskaming with a series of licensed permits, until 1760 when Britain finally broke France's hold on Canada. Overnight, New Englanders moved into Montreal, grabbed control of the inland trading posts, yet carried on Canada's struggle against the imperial Hudson's Bay Company for northern furs. And Fort Temiskaming matured into one of their important headquarters.

After the newest Canadians spread further west, they formed in common economic strength and self defence their own North West Company. But, by 1820, the wealthier, single-minded English Hudson's Bay Company talked the weary Canadians into peaceful marriage.

This was, however, at the expense of proud Fort Temiskaming which regretted having to change its loyal Canadian ways. Then when lumbermen followed by Roman Catholic missionaries invaded its remote lake, no longer could the Old Fort rule supreme. Just as the Algonquin had lost their original control over Temiskaming forests.

So this first book of *Temiskaming Treasure Trails* closes as two-hundred years of wilderness fur trade surrender to tree chopping, church building, land ploughing settlers.

1

The Light Of Other Moons

Forty-eight days earlier, Chevalier de Troyes' muddle of armed men had scrambled away from the broken ice of Montreal. Up the frozen Ottawa their sled dogs panted, oxcarts rounded high with supplies lurched behind, and troops shuffled between, until a spring thaw freed their running river way.

This Saturday morning, May 18, 1686, under the grey bruised sky they are splashing along a pebble beach, stuffing tents, muskets, gunpowder kegs, picks, shovels, forty pound food packets and leather bags into their yellow-brown line of thirty birchbark canoes. Last night's campfires a sudden storm has thoroughly soaked. Soon the bobbing boats push off into Lake Temiskaming's rough blow out of the southwest.

Their best route north lies up the western shore, agree Chief Scout St. Germain and the Algonquin guide hired two days ago at Mattawa. Then, after de Troyes raises his signal arm and shouts, "Allons-y", ninety paddles flash like wings against the whitecaps, away from the southerly suction of Long Sault rapids draining the lake's end. Yesterday's six mile passage through that convulsive stretch of Temiskaming River water smashed several canoes; but not again, the Canadians swear as their deep paddles pull flat across the current's grasp.

Within twenty minutes the five hundred foot evergreen height of western shoreline shelters them from the rain-lashing wind. Eight more hours of forty-five strokes to the minute under partial sail should speed them before nightfall to Aubatswenanek, as the Algonquin calls the Compagnie du Nord fur trading post. The three Le Moyne brothers, especially, want to inspect this frontline Temiskaming post, on a tear-shaped island formed by two gushing rivers. Because their dead father, last year a director in its Montreal headoffice, had willed his family a commercial interest. Not a very valuable one, though, because English fur traders on Hudson Bay since 1670 still enjoy an overwhelming competitive edge. As their large ocean supply ships float almost into flat-lying, Swampy Cree hunting grounds, these Englishmen can afford extra trade goods to outbid canoe-weary inland French rivals. And even though Compagnie du Nord ships similarly entered the Bay four years ago and built their own trading post, the English stole it two years later.

Now the Compagnie du Nord is paying Chevalier de Troyes to lead this avenging force of thirty regular French soldiers supported by seventy Canadians and their militia officers, to chase the English out of the Bay. Moving north with this spring weather, their sudden attack should surprise England's Hudson's Bay Company from an unexpected summer direction. Already de Troyes drills his three brigades in fighting for the historic honour of New France. Perhaps a confused history of mixed ambitions, yet one well worth remembering if you want to understand why we are here.

Go back to the earliest of Canadian times when, at the same moment Pizarro was looting tons of silver and gold from Incan temples, Jacques Cartier on Friday, July 24, 1534, planted a cross on the Gaspé shore claiming this new land for France. In search of a North West Passage to the Pacific and the mineral wealth of another Mexico, he had left St.Malo; but from shipdeck near the Labrador coast, he saw only a "shoreline of stones and horrible rugged rocks". And the swarms of Micmac natives so frightened his crew that he cursed this "land God gave to Cain".

Nevertheless, the North West Passage and mineral obsession forced Cartier back next May to explore the large gulf's western throat. By September he had sailed 170 miles up the St. Lawrence River to where a large island almost plugged its way and narrowed it to less than a mile across. On the north shore point, at the foot of high cliffs, sat the Iroquois settlement of Stadacona. Within this canada or village he found wood, stone, bone, bark, fur and hide— the tools, weapons and clothing of a stone age world. Then, without asking for Chief Donnacona's approval, Cartier tacked further upriver to another village of Hochelaga. But no farther. Beyond its island were impassable rapids. At the center of stubbled farm fields rose a twenty foot wooden palisade enclosing fifty birch bark longhouses, framing a 200 foot community square. And here some 1,500 curious people jostled the wide eyed French visitors. Early next morning Cartier climbed the great hump of thickly wooded hill behind the village. Westward he saw the white rapids toss and tumble until the broad river curved away south. The Iroquois pointed also to the mountainous, northwest country veiled in the yellow shine of October mist, and made signs of another grand river there.

Naming this height Mount Royal, Cartier sailed his little ships back to Stadacona. By mid-November, thick ice gripped their wooden hulls riding in the mouth of a neighboring river, where Donnacona, still insulted by Cartier's disrespect, glowered from the snow banked shore as twenty-five Frenchmen slowly rotted to scurvy death. Panic-stricken Cartier begged the healthier natives with repentant gifts of iron axes, pots and kettles, until they showed him how to boil black spruce bark in drinking water. Then through the remaining bleak winter, Cartier's eyes narrowed as he pretended little interest in fabulous stories of an interior northern country, the Kingdom of Saguenay. But, when in May he fled back to France, he kidnapped Donnacona, his two sons and seven other talkative natives with their Canadian visions of silver, gold and tropical spices.

As the 1536-1538 war between France and Spain spoiled any chance for their return, these Canadian prisoners stirred imperial thoughts in the French king, Francis 1. Frustrated with Spain's claim to foreign lands it had merely touched, he decided on a new principle of territorial expansion: only occupation and permanent settlement would give right to land in the Americas. Like Spain, though, he neglected to ask permission of present residents like his Canadian prisoners.

Later rereading Cartier's report in 1541, Francis 1 commissioned Sieur de Roberval to occupy land on the St. Lawrence and establish a colonial base for the conquest of the fabled Saguenay. With Cartier as navigator, five shiploads of soldiers, carpenters, blacksmiths, farmers and livestock swayed across the Atlantic. Anchored off Stadacona in mid August, Cartier, even after a six year absence, had to face scowls and spit. Nine discreet miles farther up river at Cap Rouge, the settlers rowed to shore for a rough winter, so brutally cold that the livestock galloped across ice ridges trying to climb back on to the boats. Yet before abandoning their windswept hovels on a warmer June 8, Cartier had his men scale the nearby cliff-face to bag samples of glittering gold and diamonds. Soon, after meeting Roberval with three more settlement shiploads in St. Johns' harbour, Newfoundland, Cartier refused to stay another winter. Roberval, though, carried on alone to shiver at Cap Rouge. And without knowing the winter remedy for scurvy, fifty of his men died. Finally, unable to pass Hochelaga's springtime rapids, Roberval, too, beat a way back to France.

After jewellers ridiculed Cartier's gold and diamonds as worthless iron pyrites and quartz, the whole idea of Canadian treasure seemed more of a fool's dream. What did Canada offer? A murderous winter, hateful natives and nothing of trade value. Moreover, even if the western sea did exist beyond Hochelaga, why yearn for something impossible to reach?

However, Canada's ridiculous image did not discourage European fishermen from trawling its coastal shallows in ever increasing numbers. At Tadoussac, below the mounded hill at the mouth of the Saguenay River, Spanish Basques had even built a whale fishery. And all the fishermen were earning extra money trading for Canadian beaver pelts.

European fashions were boosting the popularity of wide brimmed, fur felt hats, especially beaver fur hats. Since Europe had trapped its last beaver, the fishermen now found a new supply and one of excellent quality, for the native's body sweat and the wood smoke from their lodges loosened the long guard hairs, leaving soft downy underfur on their sleeping robes. To have such ready-made luxury, European buyers would pay thirty dollars, easy wealth for an enterprising fisherman who had given a native less than a dollar's worth of steel fish hooks, glass beads, a metal mirror or knife. Just one copper or iron cooking pot bought several choice beaver skins. By the 1590's, hundreds of European traders arrived for the feast. And eager to move into the iron age, more and more innocent natives met them at Tadoussac.

Canada Lands - 1570 -

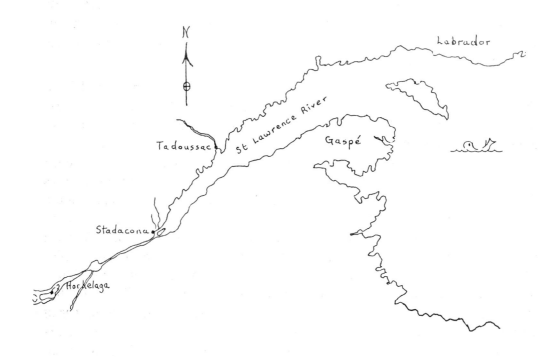

Yet as increasing competition drove fur prices skywards, the French traders complained their profits were disappearing. What right, they asked, had the English, Spanish and Portuguese traders to be in Canada? France was here first. So Henry 1V of France granted Pierre de Chauvin a trading monopoly on condition he build a fortified settlement to establish legitimate claim to Canada. Chauvin did manage to keep a post open at Tadoussac during the 1600-1 winter but his health failed. And with his death in 1602 the monopoly transferred to Aymar de Chaste, who appointed the Breton sea captain François de Pontgrave to lead a 1603 fur trading expedition, along with thirty-six year old Samuel de Champlain, to survey settlement possibilities in the St. Lawrence valley. By June, Champlain had passed all the way upriver to the abandoned Hochelaga site before he realized the Iroquois had deserted their grassy meadows, abundant hardwood forests and black, fertile soil. Algonquin hunters, whom he met from beyond the rapids, though, filled him with tales of great western lakes, a gigantic waterfall and salt sea; but nervously they warned him of their still powerful Iroquois enemy, the confederacy of Mohawk, Oneida, Onondaga, Cayuga, and Seneca nations. South of the St. Lawrence these agricultural tribes tilled land around another river flowing to the Atlantic.

The next fur trader, Pierre Du Gua de Monts, called on Champlain's enthusiasm for another 1604 expedition to Canada. In return for a ten year monopoly, de Monts had agreed to settle a colony, explore the country, search for minerals and convert the natives to Christianity. On March 7, Champlain set his two ships and 120 men for the warmer Atlantic coast south of the cruel St. Lawrence winter. On an island up the Ste. Croix River on the north side of a long, fat pocket of bay, he hewed logs for the warmer post. Yet, during six winter months, thirty-five of seventy-nine men could not escape the black scurvy death. Welcoming his ships' spring return, Champlain charted the Atlantic coast into the summer south. In August, however, back to last winter's killer bay he went; but on the opposite, more sheltered side he built the cheerier, kindlier post of Port Royal. Then before snow fouled their sails, the ships, loaded with last season's few furs, set their compasses for the open sea and home.

France, in 1607, impatiently cancelled de Monts' roaming monopoly but Champlain had him ask for a one year extension, with another promise of definitely settling a legal claim to fur-bearing Canada at the abandoned Stadacona site. "Let the English have their own colony in sunny Virginia," Champlain said, "we will resume France's honourable search for the North West Passage." To sate de Monts' need for personal profit, Champlain reminded him that Stadacona, farther up river than Tadoussac, would give him first pick of precious furs brought down river from interior lands. Furthermore, if de Monts offered the native hunters military help in their traditional war against the Iroquois Confederacy, they would certainly show more trading friendship. So, in April, 1608, a determined Samuel de Champlain again set sail for the canada of Stadacona, the river spot the natives called Kebec, "the narrowing of the waters". And on July 3, he stabbed his fleur-de-lis flagpole into the brown shoreline soil of Canada's first permanent colony.

Below the great rocky cliffs his workmen pit-sawed timber for three, two-storey buildings and a dovecote towering in the middle. A balcony wrapped around the second-storey level; loop holes for guns pierced its curving wall. A fifteen foot wide, six foot deep moat with drawbridge, fenced in by a further palisade of tall stakes, protected the Habitation against attack. Besides building the storehouse, their own dwelling and Champlain's house, the workmen cleared and dug a patch of ground for Champlain's garden. And they lifted the French flag to a mast over his roof.

Relentless winter, though, so blackened their underfed bodies that only eight of the twenty-two men survived.

Still alive next summer to row his ship's boat farther up the St. Lawrence, Champlain hailed a Huron-Algonquin-Montagnais flotilla of three hundred warpainted men rushing to kill the Mohawk, the most militant of Iroquois nations. The Hurons were a strong, agricultural tribe of traders from the Great Lakes region. For deerskins and beaver pelts, they customarily bartered corn and meal with the northern Cree, western Ojibway, eastern Montagnais, and scattered bands of Algonquin footloose in the northern middle. These nomadic hunting tribes willingly accepted the Hurons' new middleman role in buying their furs and later selling them to the French traders. One thousand miles from the Canadian Interior down the Grand River, the Hurons paddled and portaged each summer, through the final Algonquin tollgate to the St. Lawrence and Tadoussac. To sustain themselves on any of these aching trips, only the Hurons had enough food reserves, precooked corn and fish. Enough food that when necessary they could detour another two thousand miles through the northerly Temiskaming-Montagnais territories and down the St. Maurice or Saguenay rivers.

Now these northern warriors were asking for help, and desperate for their fur trade co-operation, Champlain volunteered. South of the St. Lawrence up a tributary river past the rapids, they glided to a long carrot shaped lake, which Champlain would later name after himself. To its far end they went, portaged into a smaller lake and then another river, which the natives said ran down into the ocean. Unknown to Champlain, this river's length Henry Hudson in his English ship, *Half Moon*, six weeks later would explore from the Atlantic coast.

As daylight faded on July 9 they met the Iroquois. Throwing taunts all night from behind fires eager for torture victims, the two sides faced one another at dawn. Champlain and his two soldiers, dressed in gleaming steel breast plates and plumed helmets, with arquebuses thundering, killed three Mohawk chieftains and stampeded other shrieking warriors. Though elated by victory, Champlain thought better of pursuing them further south into new lands still unknown even to the Dutch or the Pilgrim fathers. And he already suspected the Iroquois would never forgive this French interference in native affairs.

Regardless, next year after they again fought alongside one another, the French and Hurons exchanged praise and young boys who were to learn and later teach respect for each other's social ways. Young Étienne Brulé went to live in Huronia while Savignon stayed in Quebec.

Distribution of Indian Tribes

By 1613, Champlain, still loyally in search of the North West Passage, cleared a canoe portage around the rapids past Hochelaga. The natives, whom he thought could take him on to the mineral wealth of exotic India, he called Indians. However, west up the Hurons' Grand River tributary they would take Champlain only part way. From their large island toll-gate encampment, the Algonquins, in June, turned him back only to save him, Chief Tessouat warned, from the Nipissings "who are sorcerers". But secretly Tessouat knew that once the French found a way to the Interior up this great river, his forefathers had named Kichisipi, the French could forever damage profitable Indian trade patterns, especially their toll-gate business.

In reply, Champlain hurried next year to France. Since he remembered an as yet unfulfilled promise of the original fur trade monopoly which might help him up river, he went to persuade the Recollect order of priests to send four Christian missionaries to Canada. Not altogether pure, however, was Champlain's motive. The Hurons, in return for continued military support, he plotted, would invite him to visit their country if he could show unselfish interest in their spiritual welfare. An unnecessary plot this was, though. The Hurons, aware the Iroquois Confederacy had allied itself with Dutch traders on the upper Hudson River, had already made up their own mind to gamble such an invitation for an equal measure of French protection.

Of no concern was such political intrigue to Recollect Father Le Caron. So eager to convert the Indians was he that shortly after his June, 1615, arrival at Montreal, he hitched up his black robe and left with a party of Hurons canoeing home. A few days later Champlain arrived back from Quebec with thirteen fully equipped soldiers. Facing thirty-six back-breaking portages he and Étienne Brulé hastened to catch up.

Up the Grand-Kichisipi River to Mattawa they followed, then along the west river fork to the lake of the Nipissings, south down through a rock slabbed river canyon to the beginning of the western sea. Le Mer Douce, Champlain called it. Paddling south among countless islands and finally over a spraying surge of broad open water on August 1 they entered a gaping bay mouth flanked by sand-browed hills. Huronia's gentle roll of tree stump meadows, clan villages and connecting pathways glowed green. Before month's end, Champlain and his soldiers, along with five hundred of Chief Atironta's Ahrendaronon warriors, marched south toward other lands and waters to battle the Onondaga nation. The soldier's bullets, however, barely dented the Iroquois' thick log fortress; and with two October 11 arrow wounds festering in Champlain's knee, the war party carried him back in a painful wicker basket to Huronia by December 23. After a winter rest on the twin village slope of Cahiague, Champlain rambled as far as the Petun tobacco fields and Ottawa Indian forests south and west of Le Mer Douce. When back in Quebec he felt supreme confidence: he had mapped much of the previously unseen Interior country, had met the Nipissing, Ottawa, Mississauga and Petun peoples and had firmly cemented the French-Huron fur trade alliance. This alliance was the one which in 1617 gave Canada's first colonist, Louis Hébert, courage for the future.

By the early 1620's the Hurons carried back most of the French goods to Interior tribes. Neither the Ottawas, though also skilled canoemen, nor the Algonquins, who lived closer to Quebec, ever challenged this. Busy the summer rivers were. During the mid 1620's, between 12,000 and 15,000 beaver pelts were traded annually. So thorough, up to the late 1620's, was Huron trade control, that no French buyer had to venture west of Hochelaga.

However, while its fur trade prospered, France's colonization plans stagnated. Of twenty farmers living at Quebec year round, only Louis Hébert pick-axed his acre of land at seed time. And because the Recollect priests had converted few natives, let alone colonists, to their strict code by 1625, they appealed to the wealthier Jésuit order for help. Six Jésuits soon arrived from France to build a Quebec church and improve the moral self respect of colonial life. Then, even though the fur trade monopoly had failed to entice many full-time farmers, France appointed Champlain as Lieutenant Governor to strengthen his untiring, devout colonization efforts.

Chosen two years later by Louis X111 to supervise all colonial commerce, Cardinal Richilieu decided on a major reorganization of New France. He formed the Company of One Hundred Associates which in return for 300,000 livres and a permanent fur trade monopoly would, like a feudal lord, manage the colony and send out at least 200 settlers a year. To get rid of the quarrelsome Protestant Huguenots, he barred them from Quebec, but not their malice. For the following year a combined English-Huguenot fleet intercepted Richilieu's first four supply ships carrying 400 colonists, then captured Tadoussac and, guided upriver by the renegade Étienne Brulé, starved Champlain's Quebec headquarters into a July, 1629, surrender. During the next three years 200 English-Scottish men skimmed the fur trade profits; so ruthlessly, that by 1632 when France regained the colony, Champlain's Huron-Algonquin trading arrangements had wilted flat.

As soon as Richilieu reappointed him absolute ruler of New France, Champlain moved to restore the fur trade—Quebec's lifeblood. Besides the profitable commercial development of Canada's resources, Champlain would also insist on a larger population of Canadian farmers energetic enough to grow the country's expensive food supplies. But three years later, after settling Giffard and 100 colonists from Perché on one and a half leagues of St. Lawrence River land at the mouth of the St. Maurice, Champlain died, on Christmas Day.

Without Champlain's vitality, the colony's population by 1640 remained the same as at the time of his death: 240 people; and sensing weakness, the Iroquois Confederacy had started a bloody, twenty-five year war. Wanting total middleman control of the entire fur trade and now possessing Dutch firearms, the Mohawk vowed destruction of the Huron-Algonquin alliance. No one, neither a French farmer in the field and his unguarded family, nor an unsuspecting Huron canoeist ambushed while bringing furs down river, was safe from their blood-curdling raids. Yet, there was defiance. In 1639, Jésuit Father Lalemant fearlessly directed the building of his Order's first permanent mission of Ste. Marie among the inland villages of Huronia, and three years later Sieur de Maisonneuve and Jeanne Manse founded a school and hospital at their Ville Marie missionary post on Montreal Island. Fortified settlements these became, because every summer the western Seneca burned Huron longhouses while the Mohawk prowled the upper St. Lawrence valley butchering careless Frenchmen. So thick was the bloodshed between 1642-1644, no fur-laden canoes dared travel down from Huronia.

Because these Iroquois killings were so frequent, the colonists petitioned France to have their own fur trade company, one that would see more of the profits spent on protecting everyday life in New France. In 1645, supported by the Jésuits and an offer to the existing Company of 1,000 pounds of beaver pelts each year, the colonists took charge of their own monopoly, the Community of the Habitants of New France. Together they would profit from their personal labours and share in the protection of New France's future.

Intimidated by this new colonial spirit and sorely exhausted from constant battles, the Iroquois signed a temporary peace. Still distrustful, though, sixty Huron canoes loaded with beaver furs took the safer, circuitous, northern Temiskaming route down the St. Maurice River to Trois Rivières. Prematurely the colonists rejoiced over this 1646 success, for next year the Hurons were too afraid to repeat even this roundabout trip. In 1648, they did start out accompanied by many warriors who defeated an Iroquois ambush. A hollow triumph this was, though, for, at the same time, a larger Seneca-Mohawk war party with 400 new Dutch firearms attacked defenceless Huronia, destroying three villages, capturing 700 Hurons and making martyrs of three Jésuit priests. The following year 1,000 Iroquois completed the massacre. Dead was Huronia, as well as the lands of Petun, Neutral and Nipissing neighbours.

Financial disaster now faced New France. Fearful Algonquin and Montagnais hunters did bring some furs but not enough to allow the Compagnie des Habitants to pay its bills. Then the Iroquois Confederacy, hoping to play the Dutch and French fur traders off against one another, while it took over the vacant middleman role, agreed to another peace on November 11, 1653. Yet, next summer the Confederacy sulked as 120 Ottawa and Wyandot canoeloads of beaver arrived at Quebec. Scenting Iroquois rage, the Ottawas pleaded for muskets, shot and powder. Less cautious, however, the Compagnie des Habitants preferred to daydream of their debt-free future. And to speed up this freedom Governor Jean de Lauson instructed Médard Chouart des Groseilliers to return west with the canoeists. In 1656, he helped bring back even more fur. But by the time in 1657 when the Ottawas paddled down the Grand River, now known as the Ottawa River, with ninety canoe loads, the jealous Iroquois had had enough of peace. What they believed to be rightfully their middleman role, hacked away from dead Huronia, these Ottawa upstarts had grabbed. Worse, with French consent. In 1658, only nine Ottawa canoes dared venture from the west; in 1659, only six. Though the Governor was afraid any French action during this period would antagonize the Iroquois, Groseilliers volunteered once again to encourage the Ottawa traders. So he, along with his younger brother-in-law, Pierre Esprit Radisson, left Trois Rivières on June 14, 1658, bound for the Interior. On August 19, 1660, with sixty canoes holding 400,000 pounds of beaver pelts, $40,000 worth, and 300 native traders they boldly returned. Even more flagrantly bold they were after passing the spot on the Long Sault where three months earlier Dollard and his sixteen Montrealers, helped by only four Hurons and forty Algonquins, stood up to 700 Iroquois a whole week before dying. Forbidden to risk a second trip, Groseilliers and Radisson went anyway. Next year on their return the Governor imprisoned Groseilliers, and confiscated the furs. Unimpressed by such token punishment, however, the enraged Iroquois blocked all trade routes for the next two years.

Radisson meanwhile praised the best quality "castor gras" fur country he and his brother-in-law had discovered between Lake Superior and Hudson Bay. And so persuasive was he that the French in 1661 built a trading post at Lake Nemiscau on a river flowing into the southeast corner of Hudson Bay. But how to get the furs to Quebec? The Iroquois terrified even the remote Saguenay region. Radisson and Groseilliers answered that the way to defeat the Iroquois blockade was to bypass all overland canoe routes and instead send ships into Hudson Bay to trade directly with the native Cree. And think about the possible bonus of finding the North West Passage. Unable, though, to change the set mind of New France, they left in 1662 to promote their trading scheme in Boston.

Meanwhile, appalled by its indecisive leadership and the crippling expense of its Iroquois war, Louis X1V, in May, 1663, made New France a royal province subject to his absolute rule. His minister of finance, Jean Baptiste Colbert, insisted on balancing the colony's books. First, no more borrowing, he decreed; grow your own food; make your own tools. Since nothing must compete with these efforts, he cancelled all settlers' trade travel plans to the Interior. Rather stay home and work your farms. Designed by Colbert, France's newly crowned monopoly Company of the West, permitted only Indians to bring furs to Montreal. Until 1674, this latest company would control the price of beaver and levy a twenty-five percent tax on all beaver sales. Most concerned with agricultural health in the royal province, Colbert spent the tax money to send out hundreds of settlers.

What of the Iroquois menace? In 1665 the Sun King's newest viceroy, Seigneur de Tracy, sailed from France with 600 seasoned troops of the Carignan-Salières regiment. Their construction of five forts along the Richilieu River to Lake Champlain quickly forced four Iroquois nations into a December peace. And de Tracy meant to maintain it. Next October he led 600 foot-frozen regulars, 600 Canadian militiamen, and 100 Hurons to gun down a Mohawk uprising. Now, free of travel dread, Indian hunters of the north and west could again celebrate their annual fur trade fair at Montreal.

Intendant Jean Talon, who administered New France's daily affairs, welcomed them. While obeying the letter of Colbert's law against any Frenchman travelling to the Interior, Talon did grant special explorations to discover new lands, minerals and more Indian furs. A special privilege this was, however, denied to most Montreal fur merchants who then bargained with outlaw French traders, coureurs de bois, to smuggle furs out of the upcountry Interior. By the late 1660 years, 200 coureurs de bois sleeping with their kettles, knives, hatchets, blankets, tobacco and brandy kegs in flimsy bush huts, traded throughout the upper Great Lakes.

Also, placing himself above Colbert's law, Governor Frontenac chose his own special 1673 way. Claiming military need he press-ganged 400 scowling habitants from around Montreal up the St. Lawrence to build him a post at the northeast corner of Lake Ontario. Coincidence that this Cataracoui

River location gave easy canoe access to northern furs? And avoided Colbert's well policed Ottawa River route? Even farther west this year Louis Joliet and Father Marquette paddled mosquito-shrouded canoes southward down the Mississippi. Five years later along this same southwest river, Frontenac's closest friend, Sieur de la Salle, obsessed with finding a way to China, would operate a chain of fur trading posts. The outlaw coureurs de bois found consolation in the cooler weather of northern Canada and its superior quality furs.

And they sympathized with Radisson and Groseilliers who, contemptuous of Colbert's prohibition on inland travel because it also stopped thinking of any other possible travel way, had left Canada. By 1666 they were in London selling their idea of direct trade through Hudson Bay. And the English fur buyers listened. Just as Charles 1 and the London Merchant Company thirty years earlier listened before financing the Kirke brothers' conquest of New France. Given £650 worth of trade goods by their English sponsors, Radisson and Groseilliers, in 1668, guided the English ship, *Nonsuch*, to Hudson Bay and returned with £19,000 worth of furs. Delighted still on May 2, 1670, Charles II granted Prince Rupert and the Company of Adventurers of England Trading into Hudson's Bay a royal charter. As for England's landlord right to the Bay, the King pointed to Henry Hudson's 1610-1611 trips of discovery.

An immediate success this Hudson's Bay Company was. Without birch trees the northern Cree had never had enough lightweight, three-man canoes to carry their own fur freight to Montreal. Now, no longer needing middleman help, each family simply shifted its winter catch a short distance down river to choose from an eye boggling variety of low priced trade goods —quality English goods. Even the coureurs de bois found a better deal here. Yet the Montreal merchants, the Ottawa Indian middlemen, and the colonial tax gatherers opposed any idea of similar French fur trade in the Bay: for all would permanently lose their local businesses to merchant shipowners from France. But what was the bypass difference? Caught between Colbert's rigid injunction against travelling to the Interior and the Hudson's Bay Company's relentless competition they would soon be penniless anyway.

Because Colbert did not fully appreciate England's *unrestricted* success in the Bay, Jean Talon, the Intendant, had to convince him of its real danger to Canada. In 1672, he had Father Albanel report his spying account of English ships at Rupert's River regularly arriving and departing. When one year later Father Nouvel, the Jésuit missionary at Sault Ste. Marie, spoke with more alarm of the Ojibways' increasing trade with the English, Intendant Talon sent Sieur St. Germain to check further.

Past Montreal, around the rapids beside LaSalle's former farmlands nicknamed La Chine because of his China obsession, up the Ottawa to the Head of Lake Temiskaming St. Germain went. There local Indians guided him fifteen tortuous miles east past one foaming set of rapids after another into a slim lake fingering north. In seven days they groaned up Obicoba Lake and Opasatica over the Height of Land portage down to Matawagogig Lake, four portages to Agotawekami and the final dancing river rapids into Lake Abitibi. Then west across its shallow, windswept waters to a narrow passage, into the lower half of the lake they sped; then slower between a large island and many smaller ones to go over a short but soggy peninsula portage to save time reaching Abitibi River.

Northwest within seven-foot clay banks covered in small spruce and balsam, they portaged around a sudden thirty foot waterfall, then six hours later the fast river took a sickle sharp turn northeast and its slick pull of water fell another twenty feet over a rocky bluff. Sloping rock lined the shores for a mile until clay covered all again and large poplars added to the softwood bush as the river turned northwest. Thirty-three miles it ran free to a three foot waterfall and six miles of canoe tossing rapids between twenty-five foot high banks. Another six foot fall changed into six restful miles down to an island portage around a twenty foot waterfall, which led into a long river bend to the southwest fork with Pusquachagamy River.

Southwards they turned against the current into the 250 foot wide Pusquachagamy mouth up towards the rolling country behind Sault Ste. Marie. Within a mile the river doubled in width and a short chop of rapids forced the canoes to shore. Nine miles farther a spur of rock pinched the river into a steep chute. Upwards and beyond this twelve foot rise St. Germain paddled the broader river thirty arm-weary miles until a series of falls stepped up and up another gasping mile. Four miles ahead a formidable fifty foot wall of water blocked the way. Up and around the men flailed again. After ten more miles they came to a fat lake leaking out of a tamarac swamp hiding a larger lake, the headwater Height of Land lake. And here, at the end of August, St. Germain chose the large island at the south end to pile together his log tents for the coming winter. From here he could count the Indians on their way down-river to the English on Hudson Bay; due north down-river into the twelve-mile-wide Monsipy River mouth, where on an island this same summer the English had started building a large fort with four eighteen-foot-high, 130-foot-long walls flanked by bastions armed with cannons. Inside, before the first snowfall, would be a barn and a three storey redoubt with more cannons.

As if England's settlement of Hudson Bay was not enough of a threat, the unexpected 1674 collapse of the tax-paying Company of the West further upset Colbert's plan for a stable colony in Canada. He immediately organized a private French collection agency, the Company of the Farm, to pay in advance the year's projected tax sum of 350,000 livres, then run the risk of actual tax gathering in exchange for keeping any excess collected. And excess there was, as this new Company soon rented its beaver trade for 119,000 livres to a Canadian merchant, Aubert de la Chesnaye.

Meanwhile, Governor Frontenac downplayed any cause for alarm. The growing French trade in the southwest Interior, he said, more than made up for losses to the northern English. Certainly Frontenac's Lake Ontario post and La Salle's Mississippi ones were earning taxes and money for investors in France, but little of it was finding its way into the purses of Montreal merchants shut out of this southwest region.

St. Germain's Temiskaming Journey - 1673 -

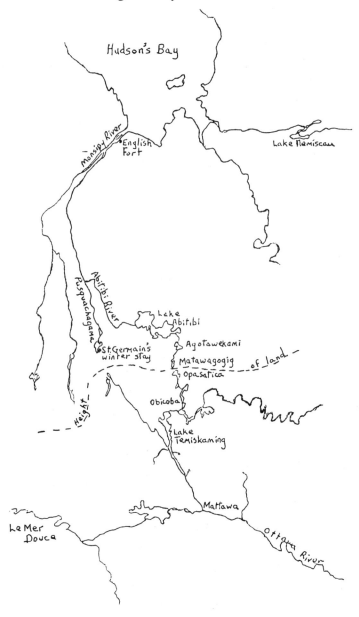

The Iroquois also cried unfair, for the Illinois tribe of the southwest had assumed the middleman trading role for Frontenac. So hot was Iroquois temper by 1680 they again declared war. And blaming French deceit they devastated the Illinois—a slaughter made most senseless as European fashion, preferring the Cree's greasier furs, no longer wanted inferior pelts from the southwest.

With their coureurs de bois paralyzed between rampaging Iroquois and Hudson's Bay Company bargains, Canadian fur merchants begged for mercy. Finally, in 1681, Colbert reversed his ban on inland travelling. He also pardoned the past crimes of the coureurs de bois and established a permit (congé) system. The government would grant twenty-five congés a year. Each permitted one canoeload of trade goods with three other Frenchmen in a second, empty canoe to bring back two loads of fur from the Interior. The new Governor La Barre would also issue private licences for additional canoe loads. Yet this was still not enough for some Montreal merchants: especially Aubert de la Chesnaye who had already leased the Company of the Farm trade, nor Charles Le Moyne, the veteran Canadian military commander and trader, nor Sieur Argenteuil with his newly granted licence to trade in the Temiskaming-Abitibi region, the same country St. Germain most recently praised. As these men wanted to combine their strengths and with a royal sponsor compete on equal terms with the Hudson's Bay Company, La Barre in 1682 let them form their private Compagnie du Nord.

Forgiven by France four years earlier, two of the men most responsible for this new company were Radisson and Groseilliers. Having helped the English settle their Bay trade, they knew best how to take it away. Proving their point in 1682, they sailed a Compagnie du Nord ship to Hudson Bay and built a French post at the mouth of the Bourbon River. Overcoming English resistance during the winter, they left Groseilliers' son in charge. But Radisson's arrival at Quebec in a stolen British ship full of English furs so unnerved La Barre he deported Radisson to France. Without hesitation Radisson rejoined the English side. And, in 1684, on behalf of the Hudson's Bay Company he captured Fort Bourbon, renaming it Port Nelson. That fall a Compagnie du Nord supply ship innocently arrived, shivered the winter offshore, then fled back to Quebec with spring news of Radisson's treachery.

Compagnie du Nord whispered revenge. And to its legitimate claim for this Nelson River land, France's royal charter granted in May gave imperial weight. When new Governor de Denonville landed at Quebec in August with 350 soldier reinforcements to put down the Iroquois raids throughout the upper St. Lawrence-Ottawa River region, the Compagnie du Nord appealed for his extra support. Denonville gave it: thirty soldiers and captain Pierre de Troyes as leader of the Compagnie's expedition to recapture Fort Bourbon. Because the Compagnie would pay the trip's cost of 76,000 livres, this was not a French declaration of war; rather one fur company's attempt to regain its lawful property and punish a double-dealing employee. If any Englishmen on the Bay try to stop us, they will suffer the consequences!

2

An Eagle's Shadow Drifts Along The Cliffs

"If any Englishmen on the Bay try to stop us, they will suffer," de Troyes murmurs as he looks around at his line of canoes skimming north like a flock of multi-coloured birds along the shore. Father Silvie's gown sounds a black note among the Canadians' red, blue, green shirts. Despite gusting rain, the paddlers yank down their cloth caps, clench their pipes upside down and smoke on. Usually they finish two pipefuls between ten minute stops but not this Saturday. De Troyes wants to reach the Front settlement of Fort Temiskaming before nightfall and the precipitous cliffs on the way offer little room for stretching legs. Fortunately, though, the quarter mile wide lake is free of driftwood and its high banks form a tunnel shield through the merciless wind.

Lieutenant Sieur de Ste.Hélène, the twenty-seven year old Jacques Le Moyne, heads the advance guard of thirty Canadians while Pierre, his younger brother by two years, Sieur d'Iberville, protects the rear. In between is de Troyes' brigade of French troops. At least ten years older than his two Canadian officers, de Troyes ordered this tactical arrangement back on April 4, Easter Sunday. He knew then only the Le Moyne brothers could best humour their rebel spirited countrymen. Paul, Sieur de Maricourt, the youngest and smallest of the Le Moyne brothers on this expedition is Company Adjutant, the regimental sergeant major. Twenty year old La Noue is his assistant. Pierre Allemand, with previous experience as ship's pilot, navigator and geographer is Quartermaster. So important are his many skills, de Troyes excuses him along with Chaplain Antoine Silvie from the daily routine of military drill. Six sergeants including de Catalogne, Chevrotière, St. Denis, La Liberté and de Cerry with six corporals and six lance corporals, handcuff as best they can the six squads of unruly Canadians.

These wild haired voyageurs easily paddle their own canoes; yet, the professional soldiers are learning fast. Already Pitre, the gunner, and La Motte smoke pipes and sing "Le Canayan Errant" with the loudest.

About 9:00 a.m. the rain lets up. Through an eye squinting rip in the clouds a shaft of bright sunlight brushes the sentinel pines, emerald green over the blue flash of water. Just as suddenly, shadows close in to gray the sullen, shoreline rocks. Some five miles on, Lake Temiskaming begins to broaden into a bay whose northeastern shore tilts up to a hazy ridge of pelting rain. The lake now bends crookedly due west, narrowing again for the next two miles, until it clamps almost shut—like swollen jaws the opposite shores close to within three hundred feet. On the right, the eastern side is a quarter-mile-wide flat peninsula of sand and gravel; the high, western shore bumps rock hard towards it. Beyond the gap, the Algonquin guide says, pours Opimika and into its western harbour they go, past the yawning river mouth to a fine sand beach clutched within a sharp curl of forest land. Finally they can uncramp legs and sponge canoe floors dry.

Here the lake fattens out to a mile. Halfway across a small, tree crested island rides the waves. The lake from here, St. Germain says, will gradually swing to the north as we make for the post.

So they follow its wider corridor sliced deeply through four hundred feet of towering rock and forest. Three miles along, spring melt water surges down a steep sided creek. But mostly the way is sombre and the western lake edge runs straight as a wall until they come to a bite of bay and pause for a chew of salt pork, wheaten biscuit and green tea. With a later break in the afternoon, along a gentler shoreline roll, they stare across the lake at a chute of yellow foam gushing out of the rocky face. Rain drops spatter now. Calloused pine trunks press upwards; frantic in the west wind their branches claw an iron sky. Long waves comb the widening lake: time for canoes to rope together and raise oil cloth sails to skim north.

By five o'clock the twenty-four-foot-long canoes swing out from a curving sand spit and keep steering outwards to the smudge of smoke from Fort Temiskaming, coming into view on a large barrier island's south side. Some of the Canadians' flintlocks shatter the air; within minutes welcoming booms echo. Hidden back west on the mainland, a lean muscular river flows out of the thick bush. The island's pointed west end, its other end swelling more than halfway across the lake, stuffs this river mouth and that of a second one raging a muffled distance away on the far side. Along the sand beach fourteen men shout, jump and shake their arms. Behind them three low peaked roofs of cedar bark slope above a palisade of weathered gray stakes. Above all a blue French flag flutters from its thirty foot mast.

St. Germain and his Algonquin pilot reach shore first. Ste. Hélène and d'Iberville's crews carry their frail boats up the beach alongside de Troyes'. And the Le Moyne brothers embrace postmaster Guillet, their mother's

cousin. Through the stockade's narrow, southern gate he warmly ushers them
to the clerk's dwelling, also used as kitchen and office. This forty-foot-long,
horizontal log house sits alone to the west side of the enclosure. A smaller
one for the workmen squats fifty feet distant to the east. In front of it a
narrow warehouse stretches towards the gateway. Passing stacks of firewood,
they step up to a door halfway along the long southern wall of the clerks'
quarters. Inside they face eight paces away a wide, stone fireplace pasted
together with clay. Orange flames lick the blackened sides of a fat soup kettle
hanging from hook and chain. A bag of flour, two copper pots, fry pan and
large knife litter the cook's table to the right. In the centre of the room pewter
bowls keep their meal places atop a trestle table with benches. Just above
head level, peeled logs, eight feet apart, span wall to wall the width of low,
empty ceiling space. To the left a plank wall curtains Guillet's apartment with
bear skins softening the axed smooth timber floor. His desk with scattered
papers and half-burned candle in metal holder, plank chair, two tin trunks and
plank bed crowd together. At the opposite end of the building another curtain
wall, also short of the sloping inner roof, hides four clerks' beds. Snug the
house is, but menacingly draughty during the icy air of winter when the
mud-straw caulking falls out of the cracks between shrinking, green logs.
Thank the cook, though, who with his bed along the wall beside the fireplace
stokes the nighttime flames.

Two-foot-square openings cut out of the west and east walls give
summer ventilation to the bedroom apartments. Three inch thick boards fit in
to shut out cold air and bugs. "Close the door", says de Troyes as he
unbuckles his sword and moves closer to the fireplace's drying heat.

Meanwhile along the sand beach the Canadians are propping up their
overturned canoes. Four feet broad at the middle, with an oil cloth covering
the exposed side, what better blanket bedroom for tonight! Sorting through
their unloaded packets they find enough corn for a soup meal, some grease
and a ration of brandy. And driftwood bonfires soon blaze for fresh fish
jumping a few feet offshore.

The soldiers' and officers' tents cover the flat clearing above the
beach to the side of the stockade. No one expects a surprise Iroquois attack
against this natural moat location; nevertheless, sentries will take turns
standing overnight guard, and tend two fires kept flickering behind piles of
stone.

Briefly the parting clouds out over Lake Temiskaming blush twilight
pink. By eight o'clock a lone star glitters halfway up the eastern sky; by nine
o'clock the Big Dipper points to Polaris outshining all.

Blowing rain next morning, what de Troyes terms "very annoying
weather" discourages any plan for an early departure. Already, though, other
reasons insist on delay. The Compagnie du Nord expects Ste. Hélène and
d'Iberville to write up a report on the post's repair, its provisions and fur

stocks. Carpenter Noel Le Blanc has started to partition off a small corner of the warehouse interior for office space. The surgeons recommend extra rest for the English interpreter who cut his leg to the bone with an axe at Mattawa. Some of the Canadians, still suffering colic from wading up to their necks through freezing Temiskaming River portages need to recuperate. And yesterday's skin puckering rain adds to their misery. Even the Canadians' mitasses, their gaiters made of canvas, are still wringing wet; their moccasins, though, will dry on bare feet. And as if these are not enough reasons for delaying the expedition, the canoes need more mending, work which will have to wait until tomorrow.

1686 - Compagnie du Nord Post On The Island De Troyes Reports As Two Leagues Around

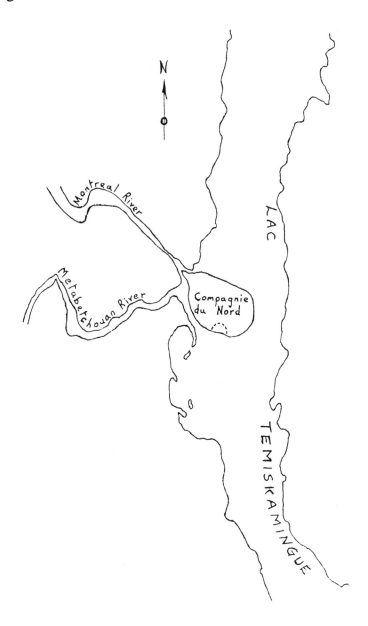

Though little bark of quarter inch thickness peels off local birch trees at this early time of year, the post has a few reserve rolls ready to soften in boiling water. With threads of water-soaked, split spruce root, (wa-dub the Indians call it), and pitchpot-heated spruce gum mixed with animal fat for caulking, they will sew skin patches over the solid canoe hull of cedar lath and boards. Ste. Hélène already has suggested, however, they leave these heavier, cumbersome craft and buy smaller, lighter canoes from the local Indians for the grueling portages north.

At midmorning, four Ojibway canoes loaded with furs glide up to the beach. These traders have spent their wigwam winter beside Wabos-na-ma-ta-bi (Rabbit-sitting-down) Lake some twenty miles southwest, up what the Frenchmen now know as the Metabetchouan River, the river at the end of the narrow channel separating the island's southwest side from the mainland. With springtime, the Indians have moved camp closer, two miles inland behind the six hundred foot high western hill shaped like a huge beaver; and so leave themselves just a short portage down steep, packed-earth steps to the last Metabetchouan length. Silently, these buckskinned men gawk at the great number of Frenchmen, especially those in monstrous metal helmets. With no less wonder the soldiers stare back at the beaded medicine bags of enchanted herbs, roots, feathers, stones and wooden images hanging from proud Ojibway necks.

His black robe dripping wet from this Sunday morning rain, Father Silvie, forty-seven years old, one of only twenty-five priests in New France and a missionary veteran of Lake Superior trips to Hudson Bay, calls for Mass. Setting up his portable altar by the stockade gate, with breviary in hand he blesses his Lord, the men and future fortunes.

As the west wind flings spray across the beach, the Canadians shoulder their canoes closer towards the middle of this low island's one mile width of waterlogged silt, closer to the empty canoe shed. Behind the island the mother, Montreal River is roaring. Half a mile inland, out of a twenty-five-foot-wide gash through forty high feet of bare granite, its sinewed waters blast into a swirl of catchbasin, then toss on in a broad fan of white rapids, tumbling down the mainland's edge. No telling how deeply the abrasive water rips through the one hundred yard length of notched gullet; certainly to canoe it, no fool dares.

Monday morning, May 20: more miserable rain. The Le Moynes and Guillet spend most of the day counting in the warehouse. They agree Jean Sebille should stay on as post manager along with four assistants. Both Guillet and Villedieu are to escort the winter's fur back to Montreal and while on their way visit the remaining Nipissings on the lake west of Mattawa, to have them build new canoes for later delivery to Montreal. The post's other seven men will join de Troyes' troop to Hudson Bay, their muscles replacing Lamiot and his three Canadian crewmen who deserted two weeks ago.

Montreal River 'Notch'

Tuesday begins in a light drizzle. When the overcast lifts around noon and the lake calms, de Troyes impatiently packs his canoe. Besides commissioning his march on Hudson Bay, the Compagnie has asked him to investigate a rumoured mineral mine on Lake Temiskaming. More than one Indian has told Compagnie traders of its useful metal shot for firearms. This mine, the Compagnie hopes, might be part of the fabled Kingdom of Saguenay treasure Cartier first spoke of 150 years ago.

Remember, the Ottawas trying to evade Iroquois ambushes below Mattawa sometimes still use this northern route to the St. Lawrence. And they would remind you Lake Temiskaming is but a seventy mile swelling in the Ottawa River, which at the lake's head contracts again and twists back east through Montagnais country into the tangle of St. Maurice-Saguenay headwaters. As de Troyes' present sidetrip to the mine requires few men, he leaves Ste. Hélène and d'Iberville to finish their written notes for Guillet's delivery to Montreal. They and the bulk of de Troyes' soldiers, under the direct command of Ignace Duchesnay, along with the rest of the Canadians can catch up to him tomorrow.

Cognac, one of the Temiskaming traders, who claims to have climbed over the minesite sits up front as pilot in the first of de Troyes' two canoes. St. Germain, his Indian companion and two soldiers sit in the other. Father Silvie and Pierre Allemand follow separately. Across the island–narrowed lake the canoeists sprint, eager to hug the eastern shore twenty miles north to "El Dorado".

Some five miles up the steep sided shoreline, de Troyes leads the four canoes into the southeast corner of a broad bay where three wigwams puff white smoke beside a small river. A few ragged spruce stitch through groves of birch and maple trees covered with May's soft sheen of olive green buds. Not trusting the fickle wind scraping the cloud-shadowed lake, Cognac suggests they spend the night here and finish the discovery trip tomorrow. De Troyes agrees, especially since he wants to buy one of the Indians' new four-man canoes lined up along the beach.

Another unfinished canoe sits in its cradle of ground-driven stakes; the long lengths of birch bark, sewn together, hang from the top rim of shaved gunwale sticks. Starting in the middle, cane-thick lengths of beechwood stretch every three feet across the canoe tying fast each gunwale side to the other. After lashing the bark tightly to the wooden rim, two Indians will line it with four inch wide, horizontal strips of thin cedar inside; each of these boards will run from bow to stern, shaped fast against its upper and lower neighbours. Half-circle, cedar ribs snapped into right angle placed under the gunwale rim will hold this cedar hull in rigid place. Knee boards are for the paddlers and overall reinforcement for the fragile skin of bark. Finally, to waterproof all sewn seams, two women patiently chew spruce gum into a salve like consistency; theirs is the best protection.

After St. Germain strikes a bargain for de Troyes' new canoe they paddle towards a small island a mile north, out beyond a bump of land partly dividing the bay in two. Since hearing of last year's Iroquois bloodletting at a waterfall on the Abitibi River section of the route they are following to Hudson Bay, de Troyes fears all mainland hiding places. And he is fast learning the flesh-hungry blackflies lurk there also. So he would rather chance drowning as water splashes in around their floorboard knees. At the island's south end, above the rocks, is open ground where their canvas tents soon rise, a blaze kindles and fish fry. While the Canadians check canoe seams, smoke pipes, joke by the fire, and Allemand inks in his route map, Father Silvie chats with de Troyes before soaping himself at the water's edge, repeating his final goodnight prayers and disappearing into his blanketed bed of fir boughs.

Early Wednesday morning after mass, fried salt pork, biscuits and tea they set out in a windswept drizzle. Within six miles the lake narrows to an eight hundred-foot-wide channel. On the right a sandy, green-pine covered point slopes up to a background hill. Needled branches whistle in a growing gale while shaded places growl in among the giant trunks. On the steeper lakeside, waves sluice over an expanse of boulders. North, past the current's narrow squeeze, white caps slap the larger lake and wind-twisted cedars make strange faces from the eastern shore.

Two miles farther they enter a wind-tossed breadth of bay; the first of three, Cognac promises. The mine, he says, lies at the north end of the third bay, opposite a large island. Two more miles across the bay, they skirt a long finger of stone and push on between the abrupt, rocky shore and an island not much larger than last night's refuge—much too small, Cognac swears, for the minesite one. They then enter the second bay: around another stone point, past low ground and a mile more of rock-faced shore they paddle to where a wigwam looms on the grassy bank of a little creek. Noisily busy Indians are butchering last night's moose kill. Two wild-haired dogs stand blackly at the shore barking. Now at two o'clock in the afternoon with another storm raging out on the

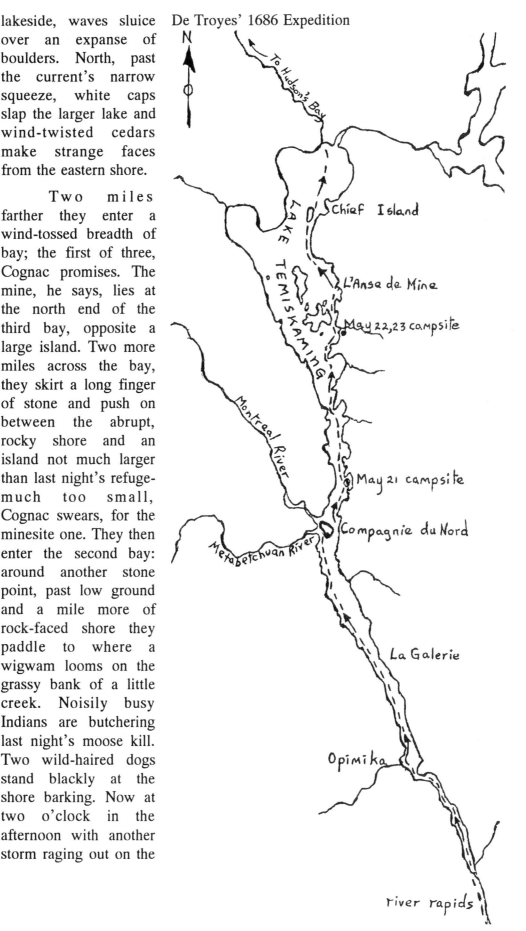

De Troyes' 1686 Expedition

lake, de Troyes agrees to make camp and let Cognac alone reconnoiter ahead. Meanwhile, maybe they can buy some fresh moose meat for a supper roast to go with their dried peas. And the dogs are wagging their bushy tails!

Naturally generous, the Algonquin family invites de Troyes into its wigwam made of slim vertical poles stuck in a circle into the ground and laced together at the top. Bark and animal skins cover the outside, while inside the low doorway, smoke from a central fire drifts up through the loose peak. Cushion fir branches, overlain with more skins, spread over the damp ground. Ringing the floor's edge: bags, baskets, and fur, seal out the weather.

Cognac, having found his bearings, returns late in the afternoon. The mine? Four miles north, on the far side of the third bay.

Just as early this Wednesday morning, for their planned rendezvous Ste. Hélène and d'Iberville have led the others away from the Compagnie du Nord trading post. With spindrift and rain smearing their eyes they have furiously paddled through the narrows but missed the bay where de Troyes rested. Driven towards the west side of Lake Temiskaming, Ste. Hélène reached a large island stretching over the lake but mistook its western shore for the lake's east side. D'Iberville's canoes, avoiding the large island's sheer rocks, pitched their way around the northwest corner on to a smooth ramp of shelving rock. Other canoes, flung among smaller islands out in the middle of the three mile wide lake, landed wherever overturned canoes and canvas could shelter teeth-chattering men. Accidentally seven canoes from the rearguard end of the line separately blew east of the large island into de Troyes' camp.

Thursday, the savage storm persists. Trusting the rest of Ste. Hélène and d'Iberville's men have found safety, de Troyes chances a wave-mad ride to the mine. With Cognac in the stern and himself at the bow they buffet north past the lee side of the large island, which has fooled Ste. Hélène and d'Iberville, three miles to the third bay. Yet at its north end is no mine! Another three-mile-long island does lie opposite out in the middle of the lake, but no mine is here. The bay is irregular and broader than it looks, Cognac mutters, as around the north-end height of pine covered rock they swing into a cove where he points to the minesite profile a short distance away.

Having almost given up hope, de Troyes will later write in his journal, "We actually found it." Then, "This mine," he would add, "is situated...west of a semi circular rock which measures fifty feet along the water, ten feet high from the level of the water and 100 feet deep. On top of the rock, there is no earth but it disappears under a mountain covered with boulders. We detached a few small ore specimens with great difficulty and returned to camp."

Though sure Ste. Hélène and d'Iberville have overshot his campsite, de Troyes anxiously sets out early Friday morning for the head of Lake Temiskaming. Three miles past the mine discovery site they slip out from between the eastern mainland and the longer island into a five mile width of porcelain calm, sun sparkling water. To the north juts a whale-backed long peninsula, its lake end a snout of yellow limestone. Left of it rounds a low horizon of distant land. Into the larger yawn of right hand bay they steer up to a sizeable island close to the eastern lakeshore. With no sign of the lost troop anywhere, St. Germain suggests camping at this island's south end. So exposed, the late-comers can readily spot them. Meanwhile, sunshine heat will give their provisions a chance to dry, and de Troyes time to finish his letters and package the mineral samples for Cognac's delivery to Quebec.

As Allemand sights his brass astrolabe into the blinding noon-day sun directly above the shimmering bowl of Lake Temiskaming, Ste. Hélène and d'Iberville shout their distant arrival. Soon the Canadians leap into knee deep water to frolic their thin canoes up and over the sharp stone shore. After yesterday's storm-tossed blunders everyone is safe! Allemand smiles as he carefully doublechecks his book of mathematical tables before penning an exact latitude of forty degrees, thirty-six minutes north.

During the warm afternoon, three Temiskaming Indians step out of a trail from the island's north end. They call themselves Sagi won i canabi, the Head-of-the-Lake people, and this island, Ogi ma mini si, belongs to their chief, his band's traditional meeting place. Frightened by such a number of armed men, they conceal any mention of their summer village, Obadjonasagin, at the head of this bay. They do talk, though, of the Hudson's Bay English with whom they traded last September. With a charred piece of tree root one of them etches a map of the English fort locations. But only a large circle smudges the bark sheet. Nothing more. De Troyes glances distrust.

While Canadian voices are skipping melodies over the evening water, the cooks' flapjacks sizzle in frypan grease. Across the lake the sky glows red, silhouetting a gentle rise of flattened land. Sudden catspaws ruffle the glowing water as a breeze picks up in the northwest and the whoop-whooping of loons warbles into tangled laughter.

The sentry's 4:30 morning yell wakes de Troyes. Heavy rain still drips from his tent, but a high, northern wind now blows dry and cool. In the faint light, canoes pull away from the quieter waters of the island's south end and butt north up the east side. Then pale blue shows through torn clouds over the wind-boiled field of Lake Temiskaming. The larger canoes plough into the open bay but de Troyes'; and other smaller ones retreat to a shallow floor of triangular pointed limestone at the island's northeast corner. When the breakers weaken, they will try again.

By 10:00 a.m. all the troops are flocking together three miles north within the comfort of a narrow, river inlet and its three low, marshy islands. Now they understand why Lake Temiskaming means deep and dry waters. Certainly in many places it is too deep to sound but here clay fills the lake shallow. And dry in summer season. Yet more secretive and calm this milky river way is, St. Germain says, than the usual Head of the Lake route farther north, twisting fifteen turbulent, rocky miles east. So, safe from unseen Indian eyes, they scramble up the clay bank, slippery from spring floods, to kneel on a weed-worn space where Father Silvie celebrates morning Mass. Soon the canoes, two boat-lengths apart with St. Germain pole-testing the depth in front, string up the most westerly of four mud-white channels. And the crimson flow of Canadian belt sashes disappears north into waiting fog.

3

The Moon Gets Tangled In The Trees

De Troyes does capture Forts Moosonee, Albany and Rupert at the bottom of Hudson Bay, but not the River Bourbon or Port Nelson one higher up the western shore. And even though this elusive prize will come under England and France's joint control, the arrangement, to Quebec's dismay, will not stop English Hudson's Bay Company ships from bewitching coureurs de bois with higher fur prices and cheaper trade goods.

In even greater dismay, however, are Temiskaming Indians. Never before had they seen so many foreigners invade the silence of their hidden lake, and desecrate its privacy. For beyond memory in every summer month at midnight under the full moon they have gathered on the low, northwestern shore. And after their sacrifice to the manitou of Lake Temiskaming a spectral canoe filled with spirits of departed warriors left the east side, crossed to the west, gazed a few minutes on the assembled people, dipped paddles again and disappeared. So clear was this great canoe the living Indians could recognize dead friends and relatives. But now since De Troye's overnight stay on Chief Island the phantom canoe comes no more.

Moon after moon the living wait till the tribal council finally meet, smoke the calumet pipe of peace and listen to the shaman Piskaret say,

War Chiefs, autmoins, warriors all our dead will never be seen again. The coming of the white man has cast a spell upon the waters and the spirits which came from the Happy Hunting Grounds will never again appear, for they know that the white man will return soon, possess our lands and drive us onward to where the sun, every night, passes from our sight.

Yet Governor Denonville vows French troops will not return to Lake Temiskaming. On October 10, 1686, after de Troyes' triumphant return to Quebec, he writes, "We have experience that, by the Temiskamins and Abitibis, the road is terrible." Not only de Troyes but also Henri de Tonty, La Salle's former second-in-command known as "Iron Fist" because of metal filling the glove of his artificial right hand, has reported this. For, in August, De Tonty had travelled with Cognac the 130 leagues upriver to Temiskaming to collect more mineral samples from the mine, the place which he said the Indians call "Onabatongas". De Tonty described the mineral as "a beautiful yellow and very hard".

Next year, true to his word Denonville directs a thousand French and Canadian troops elsewhere south of the St. Lawrence to burn Senecan villages and corn supplies. When the Iroquois escape, though, unsinged and angrier than ever, they themselves disturb the peace of Lake Temiskaming in 1688 as down the Matabitchuan River they sneak to scalp the few Canadians of Fort Temiskaming.

Quebec has long recognized New England's hand in this deadly menace. Since their 1664 seizure of the Dutch colony on the Hudson the English have masterminded the Albany fur trade and Iroquois. Back then, New England's governor of New York, Edmond Andros, first publicly urged the Iroquois Confederacy to drive all French traders out of the lower Great Lakes. Further seduced by lavish English gifts, the Iroquois, in 1682, attacked Fort Frontenac on Lake Ontario and pillaged its stores.

But during the 1689 summer Governor Denonville learns of greater reason to hate the Iroquois. Accusing France's Catholic King of harbouring the Stuart Pretender, England's Protestant William of Orange has declared war. So then a loyal New England begins stirring Iroquois nightmares of French flames devouring Senecan villages, until under the early morning cover of an August 6 hailstorm, 1500 Iroquois chop through the streets of Lachine scalping men, women and children. After dark the last writhings of roasted captives scream across the inferno river.

Enraged Canadians bayonet Corlaer (Schenectady) and three other English frontier villages—blood for blood. And in further torturing vengeance Denonville has fifty Iroquois warriors shackled to rot under the whip of France's penal slave ships rowing punishment around the Mediterranean Sea.

New England then smashes Port Royal and starts bombarding Quebec. After Governor Frontenac refuses New England's October, 1693, demand for surrender, William Phip's thirty ships land 1,300 American troops on the Beauport shore below Quebec, but the Canadians beat them back beyond the river as far as the Mohawk villages of New England. Next spring the mayor of Albany, General Peter Schuyler, marches 400 Mohawk and New England militiamen in return attack. Forewarned, though, and helped by Temiskaming-Abitibi warriors, the bloodied Canadians win.

And again during the summer as Pierre Le Moyne d'Iberville captains the naval capture of Hudson's Bay Company's Fort York at the mouth of the Hayes River. By 1696, however, while French troops are ravaging Iroquois villages of the Onondaga and Oneida, the English recapture Fort York. But not for long. Next year d'Iberville in the forty-six gun ship *Pèlican,* outduels the 114 guns of three English warships with a broadside of cannonshots which signals an end to this merry-go-round war.

Not enough peaceful news, though, is this for the fur merchants of Montreal and Quebec. For another monster wakes: the 1681 legalization of French trade in the Interior, the 1686 elimination of English competition from James Bay and the suppression of the Iroquois-English alliance in the south have together given birth to a huge glut of beaver pelts. Frantic to avoid a plunge in European market prices, France immediately ends the congé system and grants a new restrictive monopoly, the Compagnie de la Colonie, absolute control. Except for Fort Frontenac, Michilimakinac and two others, further imperial decrees shut all Interior posts. Jésuit missionaries, who have long condemned the flood of French brandy into upcountry throats, rejoice as soberer Indians, in 1700, are once again carrying their own furs to Montreal. But the bitter Montreal merchants curse losing their share of Canadian fur profits to monopoly investors in France.

Then speechless they are when, in 1702, fearful France's already powerful Louis X1V may grab Spain's colonial empire, England starts another war. New France's main concern during this War of the Spanish Succession is to hold the Iroquois to their recent promise of neutrality. But after the war's 1713 Treaty of Utrecht hands the territory of Hudson Bay back to the English Company and Acadia to Britain, Canadians feel cheated. Worse, the treaty guarantees any Indian the right to trade with whichever country he chooses.

Still prisoners of monopoly, the Montreal fur merchants are expected to stand by and watch free traders from New England take away their livelihood. When the Canadian glut of beaver ends in 1716, though, New France needs no better excuse to start restoring the congé system. But France's mercantile interests, lusting after continued profits, flatter their King to revive the Company of the West, dormant since 1681, and continue their complete trade control. Michilimakinac in the upper Great Lakes and Detroit in the lower will serve to transfer goods and fur; fortified posts will govern districts within which smaller posts will open and close as trade requires; and to lure local Indians away from Hudson's Bay Company bargains, these posts will dole out dazzling, even though costly, gifts.

Fists clenching defiance, the Montreal-Quebec merchants hire more coureurs de bois to smuggle furs to eager Albany buyers. And so great is this illegal drain on the Company of the West's profits and New France's related taxes, Governor Vaudreuil soon grants the merchants special temporary trading permits. With such a 1720 licence Paul Guillet is able to breathe legal life back into the fur trade on Lake Temiskaming.

Thirty-four years ago this May his father had to leave the post on the island bulging out from Montreal River mouth. Now Paul stares at a 100 foot square, gap-toothed line of broken poles surrounding a jumble of charred logs where houses once stood. And waves wash over the old clearing beside the ruined stockade. With most of the island's pine trees long chopped down for buildings and fuel, too few roots bind the loose silted soil and its sand bar shallows. What the Matabitchuan and Montreal rivers have dumped and vegetation anchored over thousands of centuries, Lake Temiskaming's waves are now chewing apart. In another year or two, even, the old post site may be gone. Should anyone risk rebuilding here?

As a trade route north to the region of St. Germain's old post on Lake Pusquachagamy, the Montreal River, starting with the maniacal waters of the notch, continues upstream over several exhausting miles of impassable rapids. Often, to avoid this brutal stretch, French traders travelled the ancient portage from Matabanick, from the low western shore of the upper lake to a calmer point on the middle river. So why not leave this vanishing, waterlogged island and relocate the post closer to the less hazardous Matabanick way? Also closer to the post de Troyes built, still standing at the southeast corner of Lake Abitibi. Why rebuild even for the fond sake of family memories, when higher ground at the Narrows not too far north projects a drier and more equal trade welcome to the upper and lower reaches of Lake Temiskaming?

So on the high eastern point of this northern Narrows, the place local natives call Obadjiwanan, meaning narrowed-current, another ten foot cedar palisade soon surrounds a small warehouse, clerk's house and men's house. Two of Guillet's men labour fulltime clearing pine trees, squaring logs and piling fireplace cordwood outside the palisade walls. The ninety pound winter supply packages from Montreal fill a corner of the warehouse, and Indians talk of camping on the western shore during next spring's fur trade ritual.

Four years later Joseph Fleury de la Gorgendière brags of winning this Lake Temiskaming lease with an auction bid of 6,000 livres. But to ease Gorgendière's October 20, 1725, second thoughts, Intendant Begon details its trading limits:

The ancient limits of this post were on the front, from and comprising the Rivière du Lievre, which discharges in the grand river of the Ottawa, on the north side as far as and comprising Lake Nipissingue, and in depth up to Hudson's Bay, where it is possible to go only by the River Monsony or Monsipy, which discharges into the sea the head of the said bay. The height of land is at the Rivers Labyrinth and Tabitibis sixty leagues from Lake Temiscamingue. At this portage is a post for trading with the Indians of the environs and those of Hudson's Bay, who comes up the River Monsipy. The course of this river to the ocean is about eighty leagues.

This is the most advanced post towards Hudson's Bay, the French, in order not to expose themselves to the insults of savages who may be in the pay of the English on Hudson's Bay, where Fort Monsipy is situated, do not go further for fur trading. This is the only river of this post which conducts to Hudson's Bay.

When Gorgendière, however, is unable to pay all of next year's fee the Governor must cancel his lease. But not without regret. In an October 15, 1730 letter to France's colonial ministry, Governor Beauharnois and Intendant Hoquart are still pleading Le Sieur Gorgendière's honest case. After only his first year, they argue, the compulsory presents and credit given to local natives left the Temiskaming operation in debt. The writers suggest since ''one or even two years' possession of a post give no chance of profit, he ought to be relieved from the obligation to pay 200 livres for goods furnished from the King's stores.'' That Paul Guillet and Louis Charly Saint-Ange successfully bid for the 1727 permit for only 4,000 livres a year shows someone sympathizes—or no one else dares bid. Then, ten years later Nicolas Lanoullier de Boisclerc takes his turn risking money on these ancient limits. Hesitantly, though.

For, six years earlier, Pierre Gaultier de La Verendrye set out seeking an overland Canadian route to the western sea, and as he blazed his way, Montreal traders trailed behind into ever richer fur country. At the same time, New France was strengthening its lumber, iron and shipbuilding industries. Promising a steady output of cast-iron pots, stoves, plowshares, mortars and bullets by 1742, iron mines and forges today are rumbling beside the St. Maurice River. Despite this larger world, Boisclerc does see good money in Temiskaming.

But money alone counts for little in 1743 when the long peace between France and Britain shatters into a War of the Austrian Succession. Very soon, while Canadian militiamen and Algonquin allies are harassing English settlements from Albany to Boston, British warships are blockading the Gulf of St. Lawrence. Yet on March 26, with an auction bid of 5,600 livres, Paul Guillet returns to the Temiskaming Post and pledges military resistance in the north. Governor Beauharnois applauds his patriotism in an October 8, 1744 letter to Count de Maurepas:

In regards to the posts the English have established on this side in the direction of Temiskaming and which his Majesty has been pleased to have me 'neutralize' or to utterly destroy if possible. Have instructed Sieur Guillet, who farms the post of Temiscaming and has gained the good opinion of all the natives thereabouts, to prevail on them to plan during winter for a spring attack of Fort Rupert and all others on the Bay.

And just as soon as Lake Temiskaming ice melts, another party of Frenchmen and Indians under officer command, Beauharnois promises, ''will lead a simultaneous attack.'' The solid British naval blockade, however, forces the Governor on June 18 to cancel his plans: there are not sufficient campaign supplies in the King's Quebec storehouse.

Part of N. Bellen Map - 1744 -

By 1747 the Canadians are so much shorter of supplies and trade goods, that even their Indian allies are turning to the English for fair prices. Nevertheless, desperate to find cash for the faltering St. Maurice iron works, François-Etienne Cugnet, a land agent for the French King and part time fur trader from Lake Superior, takes over the crippled Temiskaming lease. Next year, though, the European war ends.

An uneasy peace follows. Virginian merchants and land speculators of the Ohio Company at first refuse to return Ohio Valley lands taken from the French last year. Not until 1752 can Governor Dusquesne send 300 Ottawa, Saulteaux and Canadian militiamen along with 2,000 French troops to scare off the English. A twenty-two year old New England officer, George Washington leads a counter attack two years later but ends up in jail at Fort Necessity.

To discourage other English stubbornness, France claims all lands north of Lake Superior and builds, in 1751, Fort-à-la-Carpe on the Albany River. And after Cree allies destroy the Hudson's Bay Company's neighbouring outpost of Henley House in 1755, no British traders dare walk the Interior west of Montreal, the most valuable fur grounds on or near the headwaters of all major rivers flowing into Hudson Bay.

Province of Quebec - 1763 -

Unable to pretend indifference any longer, Britain finally declares all-out war next May 1. Yet despite its grain crop failures this year and next, New France wins the battles. So many that, in 1758, Britain's latest Prime Minister William Pitt pledges no more defeats. Forever, he promises to end French rule in North America. In surprise attack British troops burn Fort Frontenac, along with its ships and supplies. Then, after New England promises them the Ohio land, Quebec's Indian allies switch sides. In 1759, Britain launches a massive three pronged attack: two hundred ships carrying 8,500 soldiers sail up the St. Lawrence to bombard Quebec; another British army marches north through Lake Champlain territory; and a third army tramps alongside Lake Ontario down the St. Lawrence towards Montreal. On September 13, Quebec Citadel falls to Wolfe's Redcoats who find an unguarded nighttime path up through the cliff face. Next September, 1760, Governor Vaudreuil at Montreal officially surrenders New France.

After the sudden destruction of Fort Frontenac two years ago New France had called all available men from the Interior to help defend Quebec and Montreal. And so the Temiskaming traders have gradually abandoned their posts. Now in the turmoil of transferring Canada to Britain the fur trade at Montreal stands paralyzed. And a gleeful Hudson's Bay Company looks forward to picking French bones for extra business.

The British terms of Conquest shrink French Canada to an oblong shaped area along the St. Lawrence River. As its prison boundary extends only as far west as Lake Nipissing's sandy shore, this new Province of Quebec loses historic title to the entire west country and Lake Temiskaming north. Yet even though its Proclamation of 1763 grants these lands to the Indians, Britain does permit Quebec free trading rights within its former territories, a right denied the independent-minded residents of New England whose rebellious behavior Britain views with increasing distrust.

4

The Storm Grumbles Away Into The Distance

Lacking their traditional supply of trade goods from Europe, and having lost their money in defence of New France, the old Quebec-Montreal fur merchants have little trade energy left. And even though now free of France's mean trade monopolies, French Canada can no longer hope to live its own dream.

But just as the Hudson's Bay Company starts gloating over having the fur trade to itself, it grimaces as monied English, Scottish and American free traders move into Montreal to take over the Canadian business. So fast is their arrival that on July 26, 1761, the Hudson's Bay Company master at Moose Fort enters in his Journal a Cree's sighting of the English from Montreal who are '' as thick as Muskettos'' on the Nottaway River flowing into James Bay. This same summer Alexander Henry leaves Albany, New England, to take over the former French trading posts at Michilimakinac. Their Canadian occupants will serve as guides, interpreters and canoemen. Three years later William Grant, another Albany merchant now living in Quebec, sells thirty ten-pound bales of trade goods to Richard Dobie, a Scottish fur trader, who sets out from Lachine with six canoes to try his luck in Temiskaming. Next spring he returns with 118 bales of quality pelts.

Sneering at these crude ''pedlars from Canada'' the Hudson's Bay Company sits back in ''Gentleman'' fashion waiting for the Indians as usual to come to them on the Bay. Spoiled by more than ninety years of such servile behaviour, who can blame the Company? Each March the inland Indians gather to build new canoes for their trip to the Bay. When the river ice breaks up, different groups start out, each one trying to enlist more followers than the other. For the larger the group, the grander Company gifts the leaders will receive. Just before reaching the Fort on the Bay the Indians put ashore to organize their final June-July procession. Most impressive is when their canoes can appear ten or twenty abreast with the captain in the center and his lieutenants at the sides followed by wave after wave of inland traders. As the Indians arrive they exchange complimentary gunshots with the Hudson's Bay Company men. Their canoes touching shore, the women immediately begin pitching tents.

The dignified Indian leaders slowly march into the Fort to sit and quietly smoke. The Chief Hudson's Bay Trader introduces each to the Chief Factor while everyone smokes a full pipe. Gradually the oldest Indian leader breaks the silence with general talk of winter, the trip in and friends. Then the Chief Factor welcomes and compliments him as the conversation grows easy.

But not careless. For each of the Indian leaders is to change into his ceremonial dress: a red or blue cloth coat with regimental cuffs and collar, a lace fronted waistcoat and breeches of baize, a white shirt, a pair of yarn stockings with worsted garters below the knee, a pair of English shoes—all surmounted with a broad brimmed lace hat with coloured feathers sticking out of a worsted sash which also holds, looped at the back, a silk handkerchief with ends dangling to the shoulders. Once dressed, a leader receives gifts of bread, prunes, two gallons of brandy, tobacco and pipes. His second-in-command, less lavishly clothed, receives one gallon.

The procession solemnly returns to the leader's beaver skin carpeted tent where he distributes the gifts. Then the Fort's trading room window opens for all Indians to buy more brandy, sing, dance, cry and quarrel for two or three days. At this party's end the Indian leaders present a gift of skins to the Chief Factor and the oldest one makes his speech, as all join in smoking the Grand Calumet, the pipe of peace. Finally, serious trading begins from five in the morning till eight at night.

By the end of two weeks most trading is complete. And as each leader leaves the Fort, according to the size of his group's fur catch he receives a final gift: a new gun, two gallons of brandy, a small trunk with one and a half yards of cloth, beads, half a pound of powder and shot, six pounds of brazil tobacco, a one pound box of vermilion, a fish hook, ice chisel, hatchet, burning glass, knives, needle, powder horn, one pound of coarse twine, a pair of scissors and two thimbles.

By 1769, the Hudson's Bay Company realizes the pedlars from Canada are intercepting most of their usual trade. So it sends Samuel Hearne to open up new fur country northwest of Hudson Bay all the way to the barrenlands of Coppermine River, north to the Arctic Ocean, south to Great Slave Lake. Presuming this to be virgin land, another Hudson's Bay Company man, Matthew Cocking, is shocked in 1772 to meet "a poor forlorn

Frenchman'' on the Saskatchewan River and hear him further say how ''he left the Pedlar Franceway seven years ago on account of ill usage, and hath been with the natives ever since''. But why shocked? And why surprised? Did not William Pink, another Hudson's Bay Company man, already report of his May 16, 1769 meeting with an Englishman James Finly from Montreal who had spent the previous winter on the Saskatchewan River near the ruins of an even earlier French fort? Forced to admit these pedlars have been capturing the richest fur supply at its source, the Hudson's Bay Company has Samuel Hearne leave the Bay shores in 1774 to build the Company's first ever important trading post in the western Interior, Cumberland House on the Saskatchewan River.

Yet what about other Hudson's Bay Company competition south of the Bay? This same 1774 summer, clerk John Thomas leaves Moose Fort to scout the pedlars of Lake Abitibi. After two weeks of floundering up the French River through thick muskeg bush, he meets friendly Indians who guide him and his three Indian canoemen to the Canadian post near de Troyes' original Abitibi location. Here he meets two Frenchmen, an old Indian, the wife and child of postmaster Panneton. But let John Thomas' journal speak for itself:

2 French Men, one French Woman and a Childe, and an Indian Olde Man who is master of the Settlement, in the absence of the French Master, who is gone to Montreal. his name is Pano. the Woman I understand is his Wife, they are of the Roman Catholicke Religion by the Cross over their Gate, and DIEU SEUL in Capital Letters over their Bed, which is Feathers. one of them who calls himself Pano's Brother, cou'd speak a little broken English, he tolde me he was a Native of Montreal, that he was one Month Six Days coming from thence, that they had 27 times to carry their Canoes which they bring their things down in, some of which Carriages are verye long; he said tho they were so long coming that in 14 Days they cou'd return, as going with the Streame, he asked me several Questions relative the Country I came from, as how many Men we had, how many Carriage Guns, whether we had a Taylor, an Armourer, a Bricklayer, a Cooper, a smith a Mason &c. &c. what Wages they had, I told him we had Sixty Men, 24 Carriage Guns, that we had all the Tradesmen he mention'd. who are at 50L p. Annum Each, that we had Cattle, Hogs and Poultry, in Plenty, and Plenty of Cabbages & other kind of Garden Stuff, He said, dat is very fine Country he ask'd several other questions which I cou'd not Understand, but neither ask'd me my Name nor the name of my Master, the other two did not Understand English nor any of them very little Indian, their House which put me in mind of a Barn, is Logs of Cedar notch'd at the Ends and let into Each other & about 4 Inshes(sic) Space between Each Log. which is fill'd with Loam mix'd with Hay, the Roof is of Cedar Bark, the Fire Place is of Stone & Clay, their Windows Paper instead of Glass, their Warehouse a Seperate(sic) Building from their Dwelling House. Built after the same manner, they are Building a New House, round these Houses they have one Row of Stockades, which are Trunnell'd, instead of Naild, Neither is there any Nails in their Buildings, they have no fastening to their Gate, nor any Locks, but one to their Warehouse, & one to the Door of the Apartments where they Lay; if the Indians were Evil minded they might shoot them in their beds, through the spaces between the Logs where the Clay has fell out, they have about a dozen small Cabbage Plants, and about the same Number of Lettuces;- they are upon the Entrance of a River call'd Woo,pa,che,won leads S. upon which River 7 Days Journey from thence going with Stream is the settlement called

Woo,pa,che,won, which is at the entrance of a Lake as the Indians say...the French Men...told me Pano their Master would be back in the Fall of the Year..Treated me with the greatest Civility & Friendship with an invitation to return another Year..., the Frenchmen, in the Winter,Quit the House, and live in a Log Tent about 50 Yards below the factory.

Certainly Woo,pa,che,won phonetically spells Obadjiwanan, the site of Richard Dobie's headquarters at the Narrows and entrance way to the broader stretch of upper Lake Temiskaming water.

In April, 1775, the American Revolution further threatens Canadian advantages in the fur trade competition. Especially in August when the Americans invade the Province of Quebec to capture Montreal. But attempting to scale the cliff face of Quebec on December 31 the Americans lose handholds in a blizzard. Nevertheless, Benedict Arnold does continue the siege until May 6 when the British fleet arrives with General Burgoyne's superior numbers who pursue the tired Americans south along the Richilieu River line.

Though free again, Montreal remains nervous. With cargo ships to European markets off schedule and bank creditors hesitant, with fur prices already low from ten years of intense rivalry among themselves the Canadian merchants are starting to discuss ways of mutual assistance. So when the American army again advances towards Canada, James McGill and the Frobisher brothers, Benjamin, Joseph and Thomas, agree to pool their fur trading skills and equipment with the promise of sharing yearly profits. Having almost starved to death in the Athabaska country last winter Joseph Frobisher needs no convincing.

After twelve years of Temiskaming trade, Richard Dobie, who still prefers working alone, decides to sell his hardworking business to James Grant on condition that Dobie's son-in-law John Grant along with his partner Robert Griffin can have a one third interest. This year 1776, James agrees. But within two years he realizes he needs additional credit to supply Temiskaming Post so he enters into a separate agreement with the Montreal merchant John Porteous for supplies.

More and more traders are recognizing the money-saving advantages of partnership. Especially those waging common battle against the Hudson's Bay Company in the northwest. In 1779 they decide to take one further step by banding into one large, loose association of partnerships to be known as the North West Company. Because Simon McTavish and the Frobishers best deal with the London supply houses and banks, they are to manage this new federation. At each year's end, after conveniently working together moving trade goods west and furs back east, the partners will share in all profits. And profits there are; for each 1780's year the North West Company ships 100,000 beaver pelts alone to England, not to mention otter, mink, marten and fox. Each of these years, between April and September, some 1,200 French Canadian voyageurs canoe up to eighteen hours a day, back and forth from Montreal to Grand Portage. The main brigade crews of eight to ten men paddle the thirty-six-foot-long master's canoes with four ton loads. The other crews of four to five men handle the canots du nord and their one and a half ton loads over narrower streams to spend winters in the most distant northwest Interior, to subsist on pemmican which the plains Indians pound out of hairy buffalo meat and grease.

Meanwhile, Temiskaming remains a separate backwater to this western surge. Breaking with John Porteous, James Grant enters into a new 1783 partnership with supplier Daniel Sutherland of Montreal. And he continues his shy barter with the Algonquin, Montagnais, Ojibway, Temiskaming and Abitibi peoples, who gather each pale spring for orderly storehouse turns. But because smallpox the two previous years has devastated so many of their families, they bring fewer furs. James Grant knows he will have to spend even more effort reaching out to those fur lands farther north along the Height of Land bordering Hudson's Bay Company preserves.

From his whitewashed log house a short distance up the gentle slope behind the Fort Temiskaming stockade, James Grant embraces the June sunlight of 1783. South, beyond the sand beach, silent canoes are winging along the sharp eastern shore past the gray bluff mounding upwards from ribbons of green, blue and yellow toned trees. So still is the lake, these colours smear a white reflection of water softened clouds. Behind him the heavy smell of pine gum from around the Indian graveyard atop the ridge is sliding down through waxy cedar branches to where wigwam cones scatter, old men smoke stories, women poke fires and children tumble over wave-smooth boulders.

Yet accident, starvation or freezing death constantly threaten this remote world. Cutting and collecting next year's stove wood busies two men throughout the winter. Digging and hoeing garden beds produce September's bagging of potatoes, cabbages and turnips. Wild blueberries and raspberries may sweeten summer meals, but salted fish, ducks and pigeons must be put down in long winter casks. From Montreal comes flour, Indian corn, sugar, raisins, beans, tea, tobacco and liquor. While Indians enjoy their fifteen day summer rest, the Canadian or Englishman obeys a constant duty to prepare for tomorrow and tomorrow.

Daily chores never end. North of Fort Temiskaming the Hudson's Bay Company factor at Moose Fort is writing of another work day in his May 24, 1784 Journal:

Wind variable clear weather A.M. a canoe came down from the upland Boat to acquaint me that they had unfortunately run her aground on a shoal ripple a little below Hancock's Creek on Saturday Evening and tho they endeavored all day yesterday, have not been able to get her off, immediately dispatched. Mr.Turnor with 2 men and two Indian lads in the small new Batteaux, Cooper and 4 men preparing the foundation logs for the new flanker, Armourer mending and cleaning Musquets, and Pistols, Leask making Trading coats, three with two

Boats fetched home the Geese and Goose hunters from the Northwd. one Chiefs servant, one cook, one Ruptured and one Lame, the others in the Garden and occasionly assisting at the new Building Recd. 60 Geese.

Later in August of this year James Grant sets out from Fort Temiskaming north as far as his Langue de Terre outpost at the head of the Montreal River. St. Germain had wintered near there in 1673 on Lake Pusquachagamy, some eighty miles farther northwest over the Height of Land portage. Almost 100 years later Richard Dobie built this Langue de Terre post south of the Height of Land, yet still close enough to attract Indian traders away from Hudson Bay, much the same as the Abitibi post does to the east.

With six Indians, Grant sails fourteen miles up the western shore of Lake Temiskaming. Each crew ties two corners of one of the oiled canvas covers to a rapid's pole, then raises the pole behind and against the second crossbar from the bow. They set this mast in a moccasin shoe to protect the thin floorboards. A twin pole on the canoe's other side they hoist, lashing both to the crossbar and gunwale. After tying the top corner of the canvas sail's loose end with portage strap to the top of the second mast pole, one of the crew holds on to the free bottom corner and catches a speeding sailfull north. With no keel the canoe needs a skilful sailor. They steer past broad bays, the scaly heights of Frog Rock, on between a tiny island and deep-sided creek to the low claybanked landing of Matabanick, the place where the trail comes out. Bedding here for the night in a cramped shoreline clearing rests them for a long portage tomorrow.

As the night sky begins to lighten in the east each man rises to cook his own breakfast. Start the fire again. Loop your tea pail handle on the stick bridging the flames. Cut your slice of salted pork. Have your pint measure of flour ready. The first cook fries a little grease out of the pork, removes the meat and adds water to the pan. As soon as lukewarm stir in some baking powder, add flour and mix up the dough. When the mixture stiffens take it out of the pan to place in front of a rock near the fire. After each man has cooked his bannock, so James Grant calls the Scottish recipe, he places his pork slice in the pan with some water to boil the salt out. Then simply pour the water off and fry the meat. His meal cooked, each man carves up his own piece of pork and cuts off chunks of his bannock to soak on the end of his knife in the pan grease.

By the hour's time they finish eating, the sun is glowing pink over the low line of land across the lake. Each man bags the uneaten bannock in his tumpline load and puts a lid on his leftover tea, to last the rest of the day.

They shoulder the two canoes and backpack their bags up the slope of worn path through cedars alongside a gully creek into bush of ragged spruce spreading up and over a rock-sharp ridge. On they go in slighter ascent through miles of birch groves, cedar swamp tangles and giant pines, leading southwest around a height of banded slates to a long thin lake, Agwasabanishing. Two more miles paddling south: past a quarter mile, west shore shoulder of greenish-gray rock, then dense woods. A walk of 500 yards takes them into a fatter, much shallower lake, Ka-wabijish-keewaga. They canoe its mile south past low, west-shore islands, through a bottle neck opening on to a second mile fringed with huge limbs of white pine. The final half mile portage runs over a sandy flat, cushioned by pine needles, between close hills of evergreen-studded rock, to the Montreal River.

West they continue around its tight bend, through a series of rapids into the top of a large foot-shaped bay. Curving southwest between high rounded rock sides they stroke against the current, stepping and towing around a set of rapids too swift to fight. They unload their baggage on the south shore, cross to the north side and with a double cord rope tow the canoes away from the rocks up to where the cat tails grow over the lip of Pakeegama Lake. Five miles northwest, this river lake pinches out into more rapids. Its half mile portage will have to wait for tomorrow.

Next morning in a light rain they attach two ropes to each canoe and tow them fully loaded through a swift water way. Next, though, they have to unload everything and backpack the gear while bent double towing. But the last portage section is as easy as the first. Then they can paddle the 300 yard wide river snaking its eight mile northern way into a sudden brief bulge just before a narrow set of rapids which run into a widening intersection with Mattawapika Falls' twenty-five foot, southwest drop from Lake Muskananing (the haunt of the moose). Five miles farther on they come to another broad width two miles long. By day's end they twist fifteen more slim miles bending in a half circle east then west to more flat rapids, around which they tow their empty canoes along the northeastern bank and find another day's rest.

By 8:00 a.m. of the fourth day, the river balloons into a mile wide lake, two and a half miles long. Rising over the encircling hills in the southeast corner is a massive cone-shaped mountain. A grey cloud rings its peak. Then two miles of further narrow water gradually fattens into a half mile width, arrow straight for nine miles until violent rapids with an eddy at the foot of foaming falls force the men on to a broad shelving rock to follow a boulder strewn portage trail.

The fifth day, the river curves west and breaks into two opposite flows. They choose the one hooking north for three miles, then east for the narrowest set of rapids yet, squeezed by a toadstool-like peninsula from the west shore. Into a lake width north for three miles they go, to where the river's west branch, forty feet above their heads, cascades into the lake. Making a 350 yard portage around the waterfall and four shorter ones, they paddle south into hidden Soweawamenica Lake, up the east side of its two-mile-long, tongue shaped plug of an island, and three miles beyond to the mouth of a narrow creek on the west shore. Here, under white birch, tamarac and pine hugging the beach, wait the brothers Donald and Angus McKay.

Angus, this settlement's clerk, has the Indians carry the extra winter provisions up the shoreline slope into a back room of the small log warehouse. Within the same stockade Donald leads James Grant into the separate clerk's residence. And over their evening meal of fried bear meat, they toast the news of many more Indians coming for credit with the promise of handing over their best fur trappings next spring.

Already aware of pressure from Grant's Height of Land outposts, the Hudson's Bay Company has sent Philip Turnor with his assistant George Donald to build its own inland post at Lake Abitibi. Warned, though, by the seven Indian men and six Indian women accompanying him of a food scarcity on Abitibi, Turnor decides on Monday, June 14, to make his winter home some eighty miles west of his original destination, at the shallow but island-studded expanse of fast water where the Abitibi and Pusquachagamy rivers meet. In two days, three men finish building two eight-foot-long tents. Triangular in shape, their two rows of tightly fitted round logs lean together against a center ridge pole along the top. Moss and mud seal the cracks. Placed opposite the door in the middle of one side of the tent is a fireplace. Although smokier and cooler in winter, the Indians still prefer their tents of skin.

Despite all precautions, their 1784-1785 winter is bleak. And even though an eight inch diameter hole cut through the river ice from which they can suspend their salt pork in the cold running water does clean the meat fresh, the same hole produces no fish when their meat is eaten. Nor do any other holes.

By April, Philip Turnor knows he could not endure a similar winter like this on Lake Abitibi. So why not continue up the Pusquachagamy River? The Indians confirm a large lake there is within easy range of the Abitibi hunters who regularly trap beaver nearby. And when they enthuse how easy it is to transport Company supplies there compared to the punishing Abitibi water way, Turnor sends one man back to the Moose for permission to continue straight upriver. Then, along with clerks George Donald and Edward Clouston, he leads the Canadian Germain Maugenest and his two helpers to this most practical location fifty-two miles farther south up the Pusquachagamy River. By the end of June a warehouse and clerks' house are sitting on top of "a little gravel hill on the south east shore of Lake Waratowaha." Seven miles in length and three to four miles in width, this lake, by May 24 order of John Thomas, bears the new post of Frederick House, named after King George 111's second son. By November 7 the lake freezes over and Philip Turnor settles in for a snowbound winter. But after noting on December 23 the damage mice have done to trade blankets, men's and women's coats, a bolt of cloth and twenty-two skeins of twine, he longs for the company of a cat.

Five days later, "the Master of the So we a wa me ni ca settlement, his clerk, one man and an Indian" arrive for a visit. Then after having seen enough of their competitor's newest layout, Donald and Angus McKay leave New Year's Day. By candle light that evening Turnor notes in his Journal, "I supply'd them with provisions for their return, and while they staid with me I treated them with kindness, in the manner the Honourable Company's servants have often been treated by them. The Master and the clerk say their Father and Mother were Scotts that were born at Montreal, they speak good English and seem well calculated for the trade they are in. They informed me before they went away that they intended to make a settlement near this lake next summer."

And Richard Dobie's return to Temiskaming early in the new year will strengthen the McKays' plan. His son-in-law unable to pay personal debts has had to sell his one third partnership back to Dobie who, now unhindered, agrees with James Grant they must defend themselves against Frederick House competition. Unnerve the opposition whenever possible, they conspire.

On April 9, 1786, Angus McKay again appears at Frederick House. He has snowshoed from the upriver end of Pusquachagamy Lake immediately south. His older brother, he says, remains there searching around for a suitable trading post site. Angus, who asks for provisions will go back to their Langue de Terre Post while his brother continues this way searching for yet another site on Frederick House Lake before proceeding down the Pusquachagamy River to its fork with the Abitibi. Claiming it will be an easier way to bring in supplies for these new posts Donald McKay wants to survey the exact Montreal-Abitibi canoe route. Too polite to speak his anger, Philip Turnor grows even more agitated when Angus tells him of James Grant's orders to give the local Indians whatever credit they want and to undersell the Hudson's Bay Company by one third the price on every article. After Angus heads back south in four days time, Turnor sends George Beckwith and William Johnson to spend three days at the McKays' campsite "and observe what fish they Caught."

On April 18, Beckwith and Johnson arrive back with Donald McKay who needs provisions of his own. Again Philip Turnor provides. Then McKay leaves next day but returns on May 5 to pitch his tent nearby and waylay the business of Indian traders. A week later two Indian strangers from upriver cross the melting lake with a letter for McKay. On May 15 with the ice gone and after warning Turnor" a settlement would be made this summer upon this lake or close to it" McKay and his Indians paddle down river for Lake Abitibi. Closer to panic on May 26, Philip Turnor sends George Beckwith, John Johnson and "an Indian who understands English to take possession of our former residence at the junction of the Abitibi and Pusquachagami river, the Canadians having declared they would occupy that spot with a view of trading with our Factory Indians."

Turnor spends the rest of this 1786 year drumming his fingers for the
return of the McKay brothers. Yet, in vain, all winter he drums until he
receives permission to visit them. Originally hired nine years ago as an Inland
Surveyor, he plots his trip south through country he has as yet not seen. Then
on Friday, July 6, 1787, leaving William Bolland in charge of Frederick
House he starts out with William Sinclair and nine Indian guides in three
canoes. They will make the ten mile side-trip visit to Langue de Terre post at
So we a wa me ni ca Lake, at its latitude of 47 ° 54' Turnor measures, then
flow on with the current down Montreal River to the Matabanick portage.
Twenty days later one of the Indian guides returns to Frederick House with
word that Turnor should arrive at the "Opatchewonhaw or Temiscamain
settlement" next day.

While at Fort Temiskaming Turnor learns Richard Dobie has bought,
on March 30, the other two thirds interest in the Temiskaming operation from
James Grant and Daniel Sutherland. And he paid in full the claims Thomas
Dunn and John Blackwood still held against his son-in-law's former share.
Later this same day Dobie signed a seven-year agreement for James Grant to
continue trading at Temiskaming as wintering partner, and himself
merchant-supplier. Back up the Montreal River to Frederick House by August
10, Philip Turnor pens a precise map showing the river-portage route to
Dobie and Grant's settlement at Lake Temiskaming Narrows.

Turnor's Map

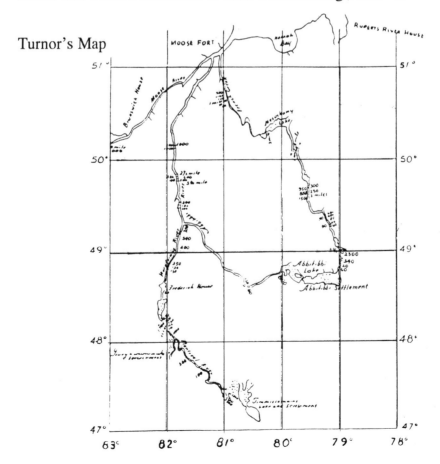

Turnor cannot forget James Grant's face turning red over mention of an entirely new brand of trade competition in the Temiskaming region. While on his recent visit to Langue de Terre, Turnor met a Canadian newcomer, the trader Coursolle, busy notching a log building a short distance away from McKay's island post. He is one of Montreal merchant Beaubien Desrivières' men, sent into the district to camp there and on Lake Abitibi. And ruthless are Desrivières' extortion tactics: stupefy the natives with free liquor, take them into heavy trade goods debt and then bully them throughout the winter for fast repayment in furs.

Thankful now is James Grant for Dobie's latest promise of more money to spend on costlier gifts for Indians. But will this be enough to hold their trade? During the 1788 winter, five different Canadian trade posts spread around Lake Abitibi. While Grant's Fort Abitibi outpost still perches on the lake's east end, he has Angus McKay set up another temporary one at the opposite end, down river near the second major waterfall. Although this western location is within ten land miles of rival Frederick House, Grant's main concern is Desrivières' three Canadian camps on upper and lower Abitibi lakes and narrows between. Meanwhile the Indians dangerously play all trade-goods creditors off against each other, until spring break-up spoils their game when all Canadians demand first claim to their furs.

Later this spring of 1788, Richard Dobie hires Æneas Cameron as clerk for Fort Abitibi. Well grounded in business management and related to Dobie's son-in-law John Grant, Cameron can also reminisce with James Grant of the parish in Scotland where they both grew as children. And they soon agree the best way to rid Temiskaming of Desrivières is to amputate his master traders, Coursolle at Langue de Terre and St. Germain at Abitibi. But their first concern this sodden summer is finding enough provisions to supply the Temiskaming posts next winter. With torrential rains drowning Canadian farms, dusty bread prices are soaring beyond reach of the poor. Yet, Dobie knows even a few biscuits to chew will satisfy the Indians' faithful dependence on James Grant for extra winter food. While Desrivières all the time boasts he has plenty, Richard Dobie wearily drags himself south of the American border to scrape together Indian corn and grease from an Albany warehouse.

By the summer of 1789, Beaubien Desrivières' arrogance shrivels. Selling his goods to Dobie and Grant, Coursolle quits hounding the Langue de Terre post; St. Germain abandons the remaining Abitibi camps in 1790. And so Temiskaming returns to politer competitive ways. James Grant and Alexander Green run Fort Temiskaming; Æneas Cameron enjoys Abitibi command; Donald McKay, Donald Grant and Peter Grant at Langue de Terre settle back to the single worry of Frederick House. Nor does the 1791 Constitutional Act disturb them. Hardly aware during the last ten years of 10,000 United Empire Loyalists and Pennsylvania Germans migrating into the upper St. Lawrence and lower Great Lakes regions, they read the sudden division of the enlarged Province of Quebec into Upper and Lower Canada as nothing more than altering lines on a map. And who cares that Upper Canada's first lieutenant governor, John Graves Simcoe, is establishing government at remote Kingston; then, in 1793, will lay out a townsite for a military and naval base at remoter Toronto portage, renamed York, on Lake Ontario. Yet Richard Dobie does talk of Montreal's excitement over finally having an elected Assembly. Too late, though, for those old French families previously silenced by the Quebec Act?

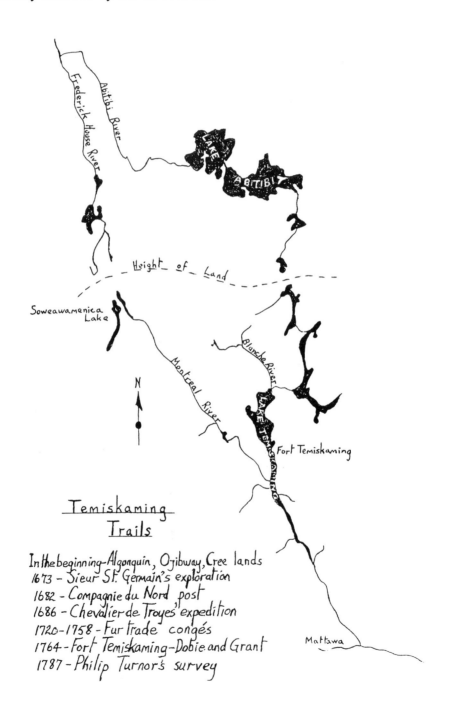

Temiskaming
Trails

In the beginning - Algonquin, Ojibway, Cree lands
1673 - Sieur St. Germain's exploration
1682 - Compagnie du Nord post
1686 - Chevalier de Troyes' expedition
1720-1758 - Fur trade congés
1764 - Fort Temiskaming - Dobie and Grant
1787 - Philip Turnor's survey

After twenty-seven years of having to balance his share of Canadian fur trade and family expenses, Richard Dobie now yearns for retirement. He sells his personal Temiskaming interest to Grant, Campion and Company on condition they take his eldest granddaughter's fiancé, Samuel Gerrard, as a junior partner. Not a bad deal since the twenty-five year old fiancé is a qualified accountant and proven merchant. Without hesitation the older, upcountry traders William Grant and Étienne Campion accept. Older they may be but not weak. For when William Grant steps on to the sandy beach of Fort Temiskaming next spring in 1792, he soon shows the firm competitive direction his partnership will take: Isaac Constant, the clerk from Abitibi, is to build a post on Devil's Island opposite Frederick House and in a year's time, Peter Grant from Langue de Terre and André Chenier from Abitibi are to assist him.

Embarrassed by such quick initiative, the Hudson's Bay Company finally makes up its mind to build its rival house on Lake Abitibi. So, March, 1974, George Gladman pushes away from his clerk's desk at Moose Fort to choose the best location. Never did he imagine on first visiting Frederick House that four suspicious Canadians would trail him all the way east to Fort Abitibi where Alex McDougall manages two small dwellings and storehouse on a point along the southern river way to Lake Temiskaming. And until the end of May, wherever else Gladman canoes among the islands of Lake Abitibi, Canadian paddles splash close behind. The best location for a new House? Two miles north of Fort Abitibi on the opposite east side of the widening river.

After Gladman leaves to investigate Fort Temiskaming, still pursued by his Canadian entourage, he meets James Grant on Lake Agotawekami. On his own way to Abitibi, Grant orders the pursuers back home but cannot convince Gladman to wait for his return. And without Indian guides, Gladman's party, impatient to discover the advantages of establishing another rival Hudson's Bay House next to Fort Temiskaming, guesses its way southward. Just as the party touches tumbling Quinze River waters James Grant catches up and together they sail down the lake for the Narrows. After the mouse-like appearance of Fort Abitibi, Gladman marvels at Fort Temiskaming's sprawling splendour. Sitting at his desk back in Moose Fort he will remember:

The Houses stand on a Point on the Et side stretching into the Lake on a high Situation, another point projects from the opposite side making a narrow Channel only 1/4 Mile across, thro' which a strong Current runs to the So-ward. The Houses consist of a Wholesale and Retail Warehouse, a House for a Master and Clerks and another for Men all at right angles within Pallisadoes. Ten or Twelve Yards higher up on the´ Point there are two other commodious dwelling Houses one for the Master and the other Mr Grant's in which they reside, those are very neatly fitted up, with printed Cotton Curtains, the Walls neatly papered and plaistered but all on one Floor, - besides these they have some detached Buildings as a Smith's Forge,(they have an Armourer constantly here who makes all the Iron work for their

Trade, Barrs of Iron come up in the bottoms of their Canoes without much inconvenience) also a very complete Ice House, a magazine but all in irregular situations, around these are several detached spots of Garden Ground, but the Sand is poor, & nothing appears likely to come to Perfection but Potatoes, which are uncommonly productive here, many Bushels are thrown about around their Houses, tho'they say they give great quantities to the Indians and are now feeding hogs with them, these besides Poultry are all their live stock. - They have other Dwelling Houses for the Winter,(this situation being too bleak and open,) about half a mile behind the Point to the So-ward, of their Trade I can gather little Information, all the Furrs I saw would not amount to 1000 MBeaver, in Beaver,Otter,Cats and many musquash, but as the large Canoes are returned to Montreal some time since much must have gone down by them, as all the Posts Ere that had lodged the principal part of their Collections here, there are no Indians about to form my Calculations of the Furrs collected at this particular Post. - The Land all round the Lake is high barren Rocky and has a very unfavourable appearance for Provisions,Pidgeons I understand are sometimes pretty plentiful, for about 3 Weeks in Summer, the season for them is about commencing now, there are very few Rabbits to be got, the Fish which are very scarce to be got here are Pike and Perch principally, but the chief dependance of the Canadians is on the Provisions they bring up from Montreal, Indian Corn and Grease is served out regularly to the Men each Day and also some Pease, but Pork,Flour Salt &ca.they must Buy, if they want it;Pork is 3 Livres p Pound, Flour 2, Mr Cameron the Master here assured me they had not four Pounds at the End of the Year to pay to any Man in their serivce. But the Clerks are exempted from any Expense, either for Food or Cloathing...Mr Grant and Mr Cameron received us with great Civility, gave me two Apartments for myself and People.- They keep an excellent Table and entertained me with Madeira and London Bottled Porter.

George Gladman also remembers the courtesy Æneas Cameron showed at the end of this two day visit, accompanying his canoe back to the Head of Lake Temiskaming. Or was it caution? Cameron has lived at the main fort ever since he had to replace James Grant who was too ill to spend last winter here. Now, although Grant is back, Cameron remains as second-in-command. And grateful for his shrewd management, Grant and Campion Company reward him this summer with a share in the business.

But no share in contentment. The daily Temiskaming struggle to outwit the powerful Hudson's Bay Company frays all Canadian traders. This summer, for instance, the Hudson's Bay Company, anxious to barter without a Canadian competitor next door sites a new house on Kenogamissi Lake west of Frederick House. Æneas Cameron, who must match this move, counters immediately with a new post thirty miles south on connected Matawagamingue Lake. Equally nervewracking is the constant challenge to keep costs down. Trying to escape in the summer of 1795, a harried Alex McDougall canoes to Montreal and hires on for next year as a clerk with the North West Company. This coming winter should be his last at Abitibi.

The North West Company not only knows of the Temiskaming predicament, they are thankful for it. Fort Temiskaming has served to divert much Hudson's Bay Company energy away from the Northwest, to weaken the Bay Company as it fights for fur on two fronts. Then, suddenly, in October, the North West Company takes a much closer look at Temiskaming.

Alexander Henry, who has joined McTavish, Frobisher and Company, the Montreal agents of the North West Company, has carefully painted his vision of Hudson Bay as a North West Company ocean supply port. Rather than the traditional overland canoe route, think of the transportation money saved, he argues. Why not buy the Temiskaming operation which already has plans to settle outposts on Hudson Bay?

So in December, 1795, McTavish, Frobisher and Company do buy the Temiskaming posts from Grant, Campion and Company. Old time, wintering partner James Grant happily retires his arthritic joints to a lifetime annuity of £100. Æneas Cameron confidently takes charge of the Fort at the Narrows. And Alexander McDougall contentedly speaks of his renewed career in Temiskaming.

Upper Canada

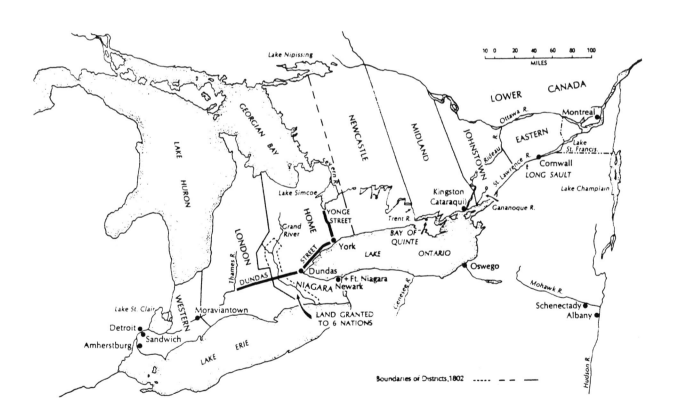

5

Let The Swift Birch Fly

Has the North West Company really bought the Canadians'
Temiskaming posts? Robert Folster, the English master of Abitibi House still
cannot believe it. Overhearing the Indian rumour he has slipped across the
dark blue shore ice to Alex McDougall's post. Glass of rum in hand
McDougall laughs and teases, by this time next year I'll invite you in for
another drink at our new fort on the Bay!

John Thomas, now governor of Moose Fort area, soothes Folster's
fluster and reminds him the only way to beat Canadian opposition is to
frustrate its every move and, until your opponent runs out of money, patiently
stay in the game. Yet difficult this is to remember: the game is about Indian
furs and neither old-time player wants to cripple the native people who
supply them; no breaking the Indians' hunting spirit with numbing debts at
the company store; no destructive alcohol. These are rules of the
Temiskaming trade. Moral duty? Good business? Whatever, both the
Hudson's Bay Company and Canadians have a clear understanding if
competition boils abusive, both sides will waste all their energies trying to
foul the other.

During the 1796 summer, André Chenier, Canadian master at
Brunswick Lake, suggests to George Gladman, now in charge of
neighbouring New Brunswick House, they both stop chasing after each
other's Indian hunters. John Thomas likes the idea. Why not a similar
agreement for the entire Moose area? Certain his Hudson's Bay Company
holds the winning hand, he coaches Folster and Philip Good at Frederick
House to accept any like suggestion but only if the Canadians will first
withdraw from Frederick House Lake and pare their staff at Fort Abitibi

down to the number at Abitibi House. A snowball's throw away on Devil's Island, Roderick Chisholm is the first Canadian to ridicule this last condition. After he trudges across the short span of lake ice one windblown Saturday in January, 1797, to hear the proposal, he bites off the conversation with Philip Good and warns him, "We'll never leave Devil's Island!"

His bluff called, Thomas next June paddles up river to Frederick House Lake and signs a deal with the Canadians not to intercept one another's Indian traders. And he gets the same mutual arrangement on Lake Abitibi. But only after the North West Company, to keep the deal watchfully honest, moves its old fort two miles down river to the long east side point of the lake, right beside the Hudson's Bay Company buildings. Up goes a new canoe house. Axes soon sharpen cedar stakes ringing the provisions store, the trader's one-storey log house with bedrooms, dining room and kitchen at the back. In their new Abitibi home, old wooden tables, chairs, beds creak and crack; the old castiron stove stretches more black pipes across the kitchen ceiling. A stone fireplace rises up the long low wall of the men's house—one large room fit for meals, laughter and sleep.

Two years have passed since the North West Company bought the Temiskaming posts with the aim of building a seaport on the Bay. Their latest Abitibi move is hardly aggressive, though. And for sad reason, as North West Company directors spend most of their present time in jealous battle for management control. Personal spites even blind them to a threat from one of their own Canadian fur trading rivals, Forsyth and Richardson's XY Company. Then so resentful is Alexander MacKenzie of Simon McTavish's narrow rule, he quits the North West Company and combines with the XY Company and that of Parker, Gerrard and Ogilvy to form, by the summer of 1800, a New North West Company.

Despite such mutiny, McTavish, Frobisher and Company still retain powerful control over the original firm. And William McGillivray, Simon's nephew, continues to work overtime strengthening its Temiskaming purchase. Just last August, 1799, in a letter to John Thomas he suggested an armistice with the Hudson's Bay Company: the North West Company would give up its Temiskaming outposts on Brunswick, Frederick House and Matawagamingue lakes if the Hudson's Bay Company would abandon its houses at Michipicoten, Abitibi and Kenogamissi. But sent on from Fort Temiskaming to McDougall at Abitibi this letter turned yellow waiting for the winter express to Moose Fort. And by the late February time it did reach there, the impatient North West Company had changed its armistice mind and planned instead for springtime settlement on James Bay. Regardless, Thomas alone lacked authority to speak for his Company's London Committee. All he could promise the Canadians was to forward McGillivray's letter by autumn ship to England.

Alexander McDougall craved a move to the Bay before that, though: think of how a Canadian post on the Moose would bewilder his Abitibi opponents. And ever since George Gladman bragged six years ago of building a house next door to Fort Temiskaming, McDougall had daydreamed of humbling this competitor's Moose headquarters. His former master, James Grant, who died two years ago bent from arthritis, would certainly have cheered. Strike at the Hudson's Bay Company's heart, he would have said, then watch its extremity outposts collapse.

During the 1799-1800 Montreal winter Isaac Constant prepared this Moose expedition to settle on the same island the Hudson's Bay Company originally did 128 years before. Since Canadian voyageurs preferred their Great Lakes' canoe trail, he instead hired Iroquois crews. And anticipating the gruelling climbs around Abitibi River's thirteen waterfalls and the two mile canyon portage he pressed the trade goods into fifty pound packages, instead of the usual seventy. Leaving Montreal May 9, the Iroquois leaped on to Fort Temiskaming's sand beach in early June to unload one of the seven canoes. Æneas Cameron told his apprentice clerk, George McBride, to exchange Constant's canoes for larger ones and see to the proper storage of Fort Temiskaming's share of the Montreal cargo. Then without much rest Iroquois blades flashed up the broad lake for Abitibi by June 11. Nine days later on his way back from Abitibi River country, Robert Folster passed his rival Alex McDougall waving a green painted paddle from the lead canoe. On Monday, June 30, the Canadian expedition reached Hayes Island within spyglass distance of Moose Fort.

Next morning a disturbed John Thomas visited, "Exactly what do you intend?" From the middle of thirty men, busy since dawn cutting logs square for summer settlement, McDougall beamed silence. And Isaac Constant, having already given some local Crees the customary pipe and plug of tobacco was pouring them a "dram" before talking trade. By mid August an eight foot high stockade circled the completed storehouse, and a few more scooped out spruce logs, their sides overlapping down the slope, finished the dwelling roofs.

Today, Isaac and his Iroquois paddlers return to Montreal. With six helpers, Alex McDougall and clerk John Bell remain. As well as a pair of very anxious Hudson's Bay Company neighbours. Since early September, two men from Moose Factory Island have camped in their own newly constructed log tent 100 feet away from the Canadians' doorstep. And in October, just before a Company sloop takes him a mile out to the ship bound for England and advice, John Thomas promises to bring back help.

A lonely 1800-01 winter chills John Bell's dream of Christmas and New Year's feasts at Fort Temiskaming. Sick of his breakfast pancake and fried pork slice, he longs for duck pies, roast beaver and plum pudding. And what about dancing and toasting another year? More at ease he is, though, the day Alex McDougall snowshoes back from Moose Fort with a London newspaper only three months old. Early to bed, up at daylight, out hunting for deer, rabbits, partridge, back for a supper of corn soup, fried potatoes and fish washed down with bowls of tea, they pass the days. And offering friendly credit out on frozen Moose River, they hook Indians hungry for food.

Moose River Mouth

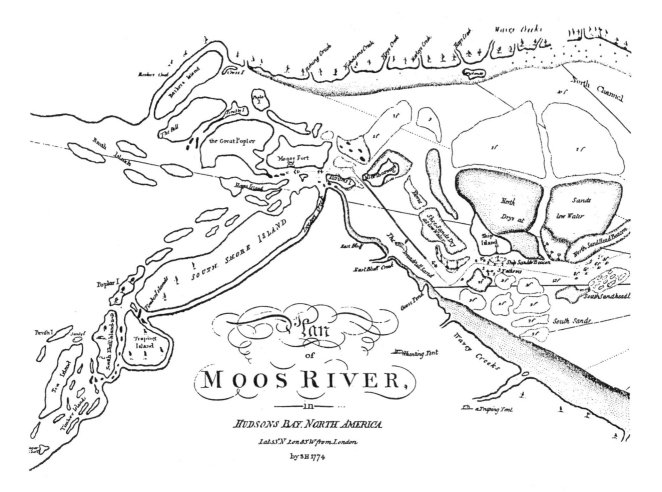

No place is the river to be in May, though. One earth shattering night a twelve foot high flood of earliest thawing upstream water, carrying huge chunks of ice and loaded with debris, thunders by Hayes Island down to the still frozen Bay.

During the summer McDougall's clerk at Abitibi, Thomas Fraser, brings a canoeload of provisions. Another load he takes in the opposite direction up Pusquachagamy River to George McBride's Frederick House Lake post. Both canoes return to Fort Temiskaming with furs; most of them, though, from Devil's Island.

Next winter tortures Temiskaming district. Snow drifts up trading post walls, buries doorways and plugs chimneys. But worse—there are too few rabbits. Indians shuffle to the closest outposts where other food supplies shrink away. And they starve. Many are near death by springtime. Once over the June surprise of seeing his newly-hired nephew Angus a passenger in the Montreal canoes, Æneas Cameron hurries him north to help Donald McKay at Matawagamingue restore the Indians' health.

With winter supplies too often stretched dangerously thin, both the Hudson's Bay Company and the Canadians need to eliminate unprofitable business. Yet neither side wants to lose any competitive edge. But despite the admission of weakness, the North West Company offers to abandon its new post on Hayes Island if its Hudson's Bay rival accepts McGillivray's former armistice offer to match post closures. This 1802 summer John Thomas does nail shut Michipicoten post, but mainly because its overland supply distance is too costly. Armistice or insult? Whatever, this hollow concession backfires as it gives the shaky North West Company a transportation idea. Why not charter former Hudson's Bay Company captain John Richards' 350 ton *Eddystone* and start shipping its supplies to the Bay, more cheaply than regular canoes can deliver?

So this ship leaves Quebec, May, 1803, and by the end of August arrives at Charlton Island where Canadians hastily build a storehouse and dwellings. To share trading strategies, Alex McDougall boats down the middle channel of the Moose, sixty miles over from Hayes Island. As George McBride has temporary charge of Fort Abitibi, McDougall can stay on the Bay for another year.

Young George McTavish, a ranking member of Simon's Scottish clan, commands this new Fort St. Andrews. Yet despite eager winter hopes, scurvy so devastates his men, they can do little trade. And next summer no Quebec ship moors in the Bay. In their own homemade boat the St. Andrews' men must catch a sailfull to Hayes Island for sparse supplies left by the last Montreal canoes. A sailfull? Halfway to Hayes Island the wide-eyed man at the tiller stares speechless as northwest winds blow a twelve foot tide in rearing pursuit.

Throughout this 1804 summer, disturbances prevail everywhere. July 6, Simon McTavish dies. McGillivray then orders Æneas Cameron to close their post on Brunswick Lake, abandon Langue de Terre but open Flying Post at Kakatoosh west of Kenogamissi Lake. In September, after Æneas decides to stay the winter in Montreal, Donald McKay takes his Fort Temiskaming place, leaving Angus Cameron in sole charge at Matawagamingue. Alex McDougall, now acting head of the Temiskaming district, must leave the remoteness of Hayes Island but since he prefers living no further south than Lake Abitibi, he displaces George McBride who becomes chief of Flying Post.

When McDougall's Indian wife and children move back to Abitibi, William Paulson, a twelve year old Hudson's Bay Company defector and adopted family friend, goes along. Young Paulson's father, another William from Mansfield in Nottinghamshire, England, had joined the Hudson's Bay Company in 1783 as a surgeon to serve for five years at £40 per year. When George Atkinson, his master at Eastmain House, went on sick leave to England in 1785 he wrote John Thomas, "I would recommend Mr. Wm. Paulson, Surgeon to have the management of affairs at Eastmain, 'til my return thro' his great assiduity & attention to the Natives last year I think him the Properest person & shall next year inform and practice him in everything with regard to the Natives." Young William was born at Eastmain, found his abandoned way to Rupert House before a lonely flight to Charlton Island and the open-armed comfort of Alex McDougall's family.

With Simon McTavish's sudden death, Alexander MacKenzie rejoins the original North West Company, which then offers to leave James Bay before this year's end if the Hudson's Bay Company will grant it the right to ship supplies from Fort York to Lake Winnipeg. But without London's response, five Canadians fur trade their winter away on Charlton Island.

Next 1805 summer, Æneas Cameron accompanies the three Montreal canoes to Hayes Island. Visiting John Thomas at Moose Fort, he reminds him of the North West Company's most recent offer to pay an annual rent of £2,000 for the right to move supplies through York. Still there is no London answer. So the Canadian schooner *Beaver* at the end of August sails up to Charlton Island with supplies for yet another winter.

But when Æneas Cameron canoes back next July he brings no more Montreal supplies. And he spreads discouraging word of the Hudson's Bay Company's continued refusal to permit right of passage through York. On September 15, the Canadian schooner *Desire*, with John George McTavish on board, anchors in Moose River. He and Æneas dine with Governor Thomas to confide they have burned their houses on Charlton Island and will do the same to the Hayes Island settlement if the Hudson's Bay Company promises to abandon all its outposts in the south. Thomas chuckles and offers them another drink. Four days later with all of the Charlton Island men as passengers *Desire*, sets sail for Quebec. And Cameron's canoe leads the Hayes Island men south away from James Bay.

Back at Fort Temiskaming, this fall, Æneas Cameron finally makes his retirement official. And so the senior Alex McDougall must exchange places with Donald McKay if custom also is to rule Temiskaming affairs. After one year, though, they switch posts again; rather than traditional pomp and circumstance at Fort Temiskaming, family life at Abitibi is what McDougall most cherishes.

Because the North West Company partners at Grand Portage have angrily condemned Æneas Cameron's final decision to quit James Bay, four large supply canoes reach Fort Abitibi on June 22, 1808, but they go no farther. Even Alex McDougall, still district head, now admits James Bay a lost Canadian cause and turns them back. So Temiskaming district will confine itself to six outposts centered on the old fort at Lake Temiskaming's Obadjiwanan Narrows. In order west along the Height of Land the Devil's Island post on Frederick House Lake, Matawagamingue and Flying Post stretch away from the headwaters of Montreal River. Fort Abitibi sits directly north of Lake Temiskaming. Waswanipu, farther north and to the east, matches the Hudson's Bay Company House on the same lake. Grand Lac, south below the Height of Land, is off east half-way along the old Ottawa River-Saguenay canoe route, doubling back from Lake Temiskaming deep into Montagnais country.

North West Company Posts - 1808 -

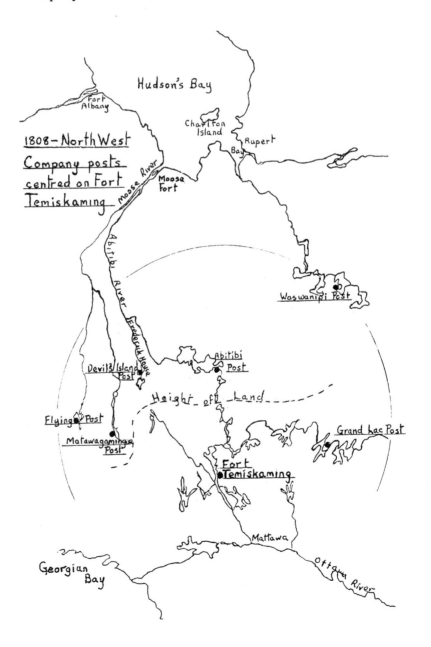

Lazy summer days at Fort Temiskaming mask emaciated February winters when great ghosts of snow spin out of the north, hurtle down the shrouded lake, buffet island pines, shriek through the cedars before the Narrows' gap, settle against the trembling palisade and wrap icicle fingers around square timbered buildings. To warmer houses sheltering within a grove of fir trees near a small clear water lake, sleigh runners glide east past the old barn and shed full of grass-cushioned canoes. But every day to fork hay into stranded cattle and rattle door locks, men walk back over the hill. As winter wears away, dining room platters steam less with salted fish, pigeon and pork as more snares provide scrawny yet fresh rabbit meat. And kegs of potatoes seem to last forever. Not the root cellar turnips, beans, carrots and onions, though. Indians still snowshoe up to the door asking for additional credit, until the sun caresses March winds mild and they can begin tapping the maples down along Matabitchuan River. Then time it is to unscrew storm shutters from old Fort houses. And let cattle munch their way south towards the little river where green fern shoots push through the brown decay of last year's leaves. As the ice goes out, some fur-laden Indian canoes trickle in and Donald McKay rehearses the post's standard of measure, the pelt of a marten. Remember three martens equal one beaver. Now is the hectic time to collect on last fall's debts and trade for extra winter catches. When Montreal canoes arrive in sky blue June, summer bursts full awake.

Again and again, summers sing of trading peace throughout Temiskaming. Not elsewhere, though. By 1810 the Hudson's Bay Company is snarling at Canadian competition northwest of Lake Superior. Costly competition it is; so costly, London instructs all its Company servants to spend less money and work harder for more furs. And grow more of your own food. It also reorganizes the Company into a Northern and a Southern department, each with its own council and superintendent. Then it declares assistance for Lord Selkirk to settle his far away, newly conceived, Red River colony conveniently blocking the North West Company's customary canoe route. Get out of our way, shout the voyageurs.

And they believe some sort of balancing justice does prevail as next year in October the water of Hudson Bay freezes early and blocks the Company ship from taking its customary leave for England. With the Moose ship stranded at Strutton Island, John McNabb, the former factor of Fort York, volunteers to carry the London mail packet overland to Montreal and New York. John Thomas accepts. And he arranges for clerks James Russell, Peter Spence, Alexander Belly and three other servants to go along. December 14, they leave Moose Fort for Abitibi House, where Richard Good will add to their toboggan supplies. But after McNabb arrives at Abitibi on Saturday, January 11, he finds Good too short of provisions. Not to worry, though, as Alex McDougall agrees to help. He even invites McNabb, Russell and Good to Fort Abitibi for a meal "of Indian Corn, Pork and Rabbits a liberal Mess of each with Wheaten loaf bread very fine — with Madeira wine," McNabb will remember. When a snowstorm blots any view of what lies ahead, McDougall has his guests spend the night and eat breakfast with him. Adding gifts of brandy, rum and Indian corn, McDougall instructs William Paulson to guide the party to Fort Temiskaming. And his accompanying letter to Donald McKay will assure them of further help down the Ottawa to Fort Coulonge. After Thomas Knight, one of Good's men, replaces Alexander Belly who is feeling ill, McNabb's party, on January 20, heads south.

While Selkirk's 1812 colony is infuriating Canadian voyageurs in the far West, the Hudson's Bay Company's Southern department keeps preaching Temiskaming harmony. So much so, during the summer their Canadian neighbours abandon the Devil's Island post on Frederick House Lake in exchange for the Englishmen's departure from Lake Abitibi. But then the unexpected happens and spoils the friendship.

Just before Christmas, 1812, to pick up more winter supplies Alexander Belly, now the master of Frederick House visits Kenogamissi. December 23, he and two labourers, Robert Sabiston and Hugh Slater, trudge back home. On March 18, not having heard anything from Belly all winter, Richard Good, master at Kenogamissi since the recent close of Abitibi House, sends John Knight and Charles Beads to investigate. They find the Frederick House buildings, though perched above the lakeshore, almost buried by drifted snow. In the dwelling house, with its door ripped off the hinges and partition wall of Belly's apartment battered down, there is not a murmur. Nor is anyone in the warehouse where guns, ammunition and provisions are missing. The three dogs, two cats and poultry have also disappeared. But after the two men stumble over the rigid corpses of an Indian and his wife in the men's quarters they shudder cold fear, quietly tie their snowshoes on and flee back west across the lake. More men return in April to find Slater's body crushed under empty kegs in the servants' house. Outside, now partly revealed by the melting snow, sprawl an Indian couple; also shot, their smothered baby clutched underneath. Later when salvaging what whole bits are left of Frederick House at the end of June, Good's men smell five more bodies: those of Belly, Sabiston and three Indians dumped along a tag alder pathway. Good declares a reward of fifty made beavers for anyone able to reveal the killers. As the murderers have left no clues, Angus Cameron promises to watch out for anyone wearing suspicious red cloth, calico shirts or carrying new guns. And he does for a month. Until he loses his temper.

For, left with only Kenogamissi House trading in the Height of Land area, the Hudson's Bay Company feels compelled this 1813 summer to build a new house farther south on Matawagamingue Lake. Though hidden behind the island at Minisinakwa River mouth on the west side of the lake, this intrusion enrages Angus Cameron, who fumes the English Company promised no more posts. Wait a minute—we've kept our word, is the answer; we are simply shifting the bones of Frederick House. Cameron never expected, however, to share his annual crop of twenty fur bundles. And now resentful of such apparent trickery he vows to ruin their trade.

Even as Hudson's Bay men are squaring logs for the storehouse, Cameron places two of his men a few feet away from their swinging axes. And when an Englishman walks, a Canadian follows at his heels. Relentless? During the 1814-15 winter, Cameron's men stand back to watch the English who, victims of their own company's newest policy of rationing provisions, are scouring the bush in search of scarce rabbits, partridge, even maggots, anything meaty enough to sustain life. Hollow eyes stare out from blankets caught under their chins, covering their cheeks and tied above their heads. On top, flannel lined, otter skin caps pull down wide bottom flaps over their shoulders. Yet even moose and beaver skin capes cannot heat their thin flesh. Chunks of torn cloth stuff outer stockings stretched from ankle to groin; so bulky are these worsted leg wrappings they conceal the Indian gaiters tied below the knees, but they do keep frostbite away. Three pairs of rumpled socks, bunching out of moccasins lashed halfway up the lower legs, protect their feet. And large, beaver fur-lined mittens engulf their hands.

Without a layer of heavy planks insulating their log dwellings, white frost blisters the cracks of inside walls. Bed blankets brushing these at night stick fast. And as more chinking chunks of clay fall out from between the logs, snow blows in to slide across the floor up to the feet of those clinging around the blackened stove.

Half starved in April they tighten the ribs of their canoes to drift down river for Moose Fort. Having to walk, though, over solid ice which still packs the lakes, they huddle for rest against ragged fires under make-shift log lean-tos. And little extra blanket warmth their flannel lined waistcoats provide at night. Around their necks sling powderhorns, flint bags and packs of salt pork rinds mixed with handfuls of flour, raisins and scurvy grass. With gun, ice chisel and steel hook, they pray for a catch of fresh fish, despite being mocked by wild geese honking a fat way north.

Why does the Company, they wonder, still insist on low rations since with Napoléon's defeat, European markets again demand our furs? Why, especially since our Red River Colony so tightly blocks the Canadians in the far West from their winter food staple of pemmican, Hudson's Bay Company profits are even increasing? And the Canadians themselves are forfeiting their own profits as their war against the Americans slows down their Great Lakes' canoe route.

In May, George Budge leads fresh Hudson's Bay traders back through blood thirsty blackflies to find Matawagamingue dwelling house a pile of ashes — an accident according to Angus Cameron's men. But surprised by their outrageous return, however frail, Cameron sends John Grant north to erect a bitter rival post at Kenogamissi, beside the English house. And more English mistakes assist his vengeance: for as if the Hudson's Bay Company's stubborn policy to penny-pinch food provisions was not disaster enough, this year's supply ships cannot break through James Bay ice to Moose Fort. So Budge receives no annual provisions at all. Not even seed potatoes, though the late summer frost would have destroyed the garden anyway. Rabbits are scarcer than ever. Fish? None.

For merciful help George Gladman dog-teams up the Moose and Abitibi rivers on his Lake Temiskaming way to Montreal. Reaching Fort Abitibi in January, Gladman visits Alex McDougall, asking him to arrest the local Indian, Capascoos, suspected of the Frederick House massacre. McDougall, though, scorns the Hudson's Bay Company's haphazard investigation and wants more definite proof. And of the present whereabouts of her accused brother, William Paulson's wife has not a word to say. By the slow time Gladman does arrive at Montreal in March, he is too late to rescue his starving traders at Matawagamingue.

Begging Angus Cameron for February food scraps, George Budge has had to promise not to occupy his dilapidated post next year. And paper-white in March he begs again. Yet now the Canadians are also kicking their own empty pork barrels and have wrung the neck of their last chicken. At Kenogamissi which is no better off, an Englishman starves to death. In late May, true to his famished word, Budge does abandon his Matawagamingue House. Neither opposition side thinks of furs: equally desperate Indians have eaten most of them.

Because Alex McDougall has retired in May, Angus Cameron paddles out to Montreal and becomes a North West Company partner. With McDougall gone he will be the only wintering partner in Temiskaming. Nevertheless, he chooses to remain at Matawagamingue while Donald McKay continues to preside at Fort Temiskaming and the district's most senior man, George McBride, stays at Flying Post. Thomas Fraser, who has clerked most of the last fourteen years with Alex McDougall, will take his old chief's place at Fort Abitibi. Blissful lives these are when compared to the far northwest news of the voyageurs' Seven Oaks killings on June 19 and Lord Selkirk's swooping July revenge to capture Fort William in August. Certainly trade rivalry in Temiskaming falls short of this distant bloodshed.

Angus Cameron does not feel kindly, though, this 1816 summer, as James Kellock rebuilds Matawagamingue House. Another broken promise, Cameron charges, let them pay for it. Again the English try to live on short rations. Again despite endless snowdrifted weeks of praying over snares, they catch few rabbits. So few that during a bone-snapping chill several Englishmen at Matawagamingue and Kenogamissi die. Deluded by hopes of a twenty-four hour a day lookout for rabbit tracks, Kellock, his shivering men and their wives stumble out of ice block houses into warmer log tents clawed together from poplar poles. By the end of March, Cameron finally doles out three days worth of food, enough for Kellock's party to shuffle down the Mattagami River to Kenogamissi.

Next winter winds, wail through the empty window sockets of Matawagamingue House. Yet happy fortune this is for the English, as rabbits are scarcer than ever and tuberculosis now chokes the lungs of local Indians. Even though the Hudson's Bay Company supply ships have pushed through ice to Moose Fort's new, more accessible location on Factory Island, Kellock has dared travel no farther than straight up Pusquachagamy River to the end lake beyond the desolate ruins of Frederick House. Umbilical cord safe here his men can devour two full meals a day. More provisions are also restoring the trading strength of Peter Spence's Kenogamissi House.

Ironically, by the spring of 1819 when Angus Cameron closes his undernourished Kenogamissi outpost, tuberculosis soon after ravages his Matawagamingue Indian traders.

A year later Donald McKay dies at Fort Temiskaming. As George McBride succeeds him, Angus Cameron must add Flying Post to his own heavy burden. Yet, nerve endings bruised by constant trade clashes, pinched by famine and disease, all of these surviving Canadians are growing brittle. And though proud of holding their competitive own for so long, in May 1821, as Joseph Beioley brings four richly loaded canoes from Moose Factory island to supply a new Hudson's Bay Company House on Lake Abitibi, the Canadians seem broken. Then after listening to a few end-of-June words they are left numb. For in spite of their twenty, tiring years of personal devotion, "The North West Company Has Sold Out To The Hudson's Bay Company!"

A complete surrender? Not as first feared. The new union may bear the Hudson's Bay name but North West partners will hold a majority of the wintering jobs: fifteen of the twenty-five chief factor positions and seventeen of the twenty-eight chief traders. Each company will equally share costs, profits and place two representatives on a new committee chaired by the Governor of the new Hudson's Bay Company. Northern and Southern councils will divide the vast fur lands into manageable portions. Both the North West Company agents, McGillivray's Thain & Co., and the London Committee holding the original 1670 Hudson's Bay Company charter completely endorse the merger.

Because he was a partner in the old North West Company, the new merger promotes Angus Cameron to chief trader. Although now entitled to take charge of Temiskaming district, he chooses to stay at Matawagamingue. Yet next May, 1822, after George McBride dies from a sudden illness, Cameron must send his chief clerk, the late Donald McKay's eldest son John, to smooth his June 22 take-over of Fort Temiskaming. Three days after Cameron's arrival, Chief Trader Joseph Beioley's Moose Factory canoe also pulls up to the Lake Temiskaming beach. That Beioley is already surveying a new supply route between this Fort and Moose Factory exasperates Angus who wants to continue the traditional Montreal connection. And he soon gets his way. For now. Even Beioley cannot resist the Saturday, June 29 thrill when one of the labourers clearing driftwood from the beach in front of the Fort shouts his afternoon sighting of the Montreal brigade. Over the choppy water seven of the canoes, each eight man crew carrying seventy pieces, land by 4:00 o'clock. Fantastically painted figures decorate their prancing bows. Red bandanas stuck with a single eagle feather still circle the voyageurs' long hair as they strut ashore. Earlier the local Indians fired off their rusty muskets; now their canoes dart around like dragon flies. Up the yellow beach within the palisade, towering seventy-five feet over the lawn in front of the clerk's house the Union Jack whip-cracks red, white and blue. Then from the north into the lake's shimmering shine on Sunday afternoon come the Grand Lac traders, Andrew McPherson and John McRae, with thirty-five packs of fur, half beaver, the others bear, otter and lynx.

Rocking his porch chair in front of Cameron's house, Joseph Beioley watches the Monday bustle beside the fifty foot long store. Already the Indians lining up there remember the sweet taste of lard, the laughing colours and ready made smoothness of wool blankets, shirts, coats.... The store, Beioley notes, is

from 24 to 30 feet wide it is very capacious and including a Garret of about 4 feet side wall, with projecting Cased Windows is 3 Stories High - The Ground Floor is in two Divisions, the smallest of which has Some Rolls of Bark-and some Rundlets/Liquor or Meat Kegs apparently/in it,-the other Division has in it the Corn Mill-some Bags of Corn and Pease,&c-The first floor is also divided into Two Parts,-One of which is used as the Trading Room-the other appropriated as a kind of Store for the reception of the Goods.One Corner of the latter is converted into an Office or Counting House-These Divisions have each an outer Door before which a covered Platform runs the whole Length of the House, and the ascent to which is by a Staircase direct from the Yard. At the end of the Trading Room-/within doors/a Staircase leads to the 3rd Story or Garret-which is, I observe, used as a Fur Shed.

And of his dwelling house perch Beioley says it is

of a singular shape being in the form of a Cross-the middle part being raised a Story above the rest, and pavilion-roofed to a Point-including the Pavilion Part it is 3 Stories high, the Roofing of the projecting Arms of the Cross is merely sloped from the middle part-and covered with Tin on 3 Sides-The Tin I am informed was the late Mr McKays own property.-Tho'the House has been erected several years it is still in an unfinished state-and it appears not to be the intention now to finish it-as they are squaring and collecting logs for building another Dwelling House.-The Store and other Houses are weather boarded and roofed with Shingle, cut to 1 foot in length and about 6 or 7 inches in width-It has a very pretty appearance-and will I understand last 20 years or more.

In the lengthening afternoon shadows, over biscuits and mugs of brandy-laced tea Angus Cameron and Joseph Beioley are fretting about the rival American Fur Company's trading post built last fall on the large lake sprawled some thirty miles away to the southwest. Last winter, too many of the Indians up the Matabitchuan River's chain of lakes sold their furs there. What should we do?

Nothing right now, Angus thinks. And since he cannot sleep nights, still haunted by bilious quarrels of past winters, he asks the Company for sick-leave rest this coming season. In a compromise gesture before his departure, though, he goes to Moose Factory to help Beioley decide next spring's canoe route north, if not for supplies at least for furs. To fill in for Cameron, Thomas Fraser comes down from Abitibi leaving William Paulson in charge. But until his June, 1823, return from Scotland the harsh news of his uncle Æneas' September death in Montreal darkens all the days of Angus Cameron's slow cure.

When back at Fort Temiskaming, his men warn him of threatening weather signs. Incessant rain storms are drowning the warrens of newly born rabbits. And even in the Narrows, where whenever a south wind blows the pickerel feed greedily on drifting minnows, few fish are swimming under any wind. So few the gulls no longer squeal there for fishes' bitten leftovers. To make sure the cattle will fatten, at least, in case of famine next winter, Cameron directs John McKay to have them rounded up from lean bush meanderings and herded south down to the thick grass of Little River. But when the annual pigeons flock like a late snowfall onto local raspberry patches the talk of winter food shortages seems false. And the Indians, who will not salt away even pigeon meat for a hungrier day, who trust in trapping their winter food fresh, laugh. Yet remembering empty Matawagamingue stomachs, Angus Cameron further directs three men to harvest the Indian haylands at the head of Lake Temiskaming. He places John Loutitt in charge. No stranger to starvation, Loutitt seven years ago fled George Budge's desperate winter clumsiness at Matawagamingue House and joined the Canadians. By this present summer's end his men have hewn a barn with stables and have ploughed the surrounding fields for grain. In thanks for an outpost nearby stocked with such provisions, the Indian villagers at the Head of the Lake helped the barn builders by piling moss and rotten wood onto smudge fires to drive mosquitoes away.

Loutitt's men paddle back to the Narrows to ship eight head of cattle up to the New Farm. But steady northern winds creasing the broad lake force the men into shoulder harness to tow the boat loads back along the western shore, up around Wabi's Bay, Wabi's Point and on to the Head. Hobbled to their knees, the seasick animals bellow over the roll of waves smashing against the 300 foot high face of Frog Rock. At its heaving base an Indian throws tobacco to calm troubled spirits. Farther north the first consistently rock-free mile of shoreline contains Matabanick where a series of six gurgling streams, each 500 feet apart, cut down from the top of the horizon ridge through the dense forest of white birch, poplar, balsam, spruce, pine and cedar. Bent low up till now from clambering over sharp, slippery rocks, Loutitt's men can simply splash through a wash of granite-bouldered, limestone-littered beach. White birch groves along the hillside give way to choking clumps of stream-edge cedars. Around a northern bump of limestone point they leave Matabanick, on four miles more to the sluggish, clay-banked river entrance-way into the Wabikijick family hunting grounds. Then, at last, within the shelter of the lake's northern shore, they paddle and tow the remaining miles east to New Farm.

Angus Cameron and Thomas Fraser, who has stayed on for the busy summer months at Fort Temiskaming, eat apart from the clerks and set a sparse table to test how long a survival diet of a keg of pork, bag of flour, twenty-five pounds of sugar, twenty-nine of butter, five of grease, and two pounds of tea can sustain two men for corresponding winter months until June canoes arrive from Montreal. And salvation practice this is, for in the real spine chill of winter, Indians will later cry for potatoes and fish. Those at the Head of the Lake come closest to starvation; only an early March thaw saves them as maple syrup begins to boil.

As soon as soil softens to April mud, Angus Cameron speeds two men up the lake to sow corn and barley, to plant potatoes at New Farm. Two others, their hands caked with dirt, remain behind clearing more garden space across the Narrows up slope from the south bayshore crescent. Why the haste? Remembering his Matawagamingue days, Cameron knows that few rabbits in the diseased bush means few edible offspring for next winter. Amazingly, though, in June, in spite of little food this winter ended, Temiskaming Indians carry almost 200 packs of fur out of the bush.

But next 1824-25 winter is savagely worse. Some Indians at Matawagamingue starve to death. And tormented rumours of Windigo cannibalism seep out of the Head of Lake Temiskaming. No one has muscle enough to crawl around a trapline.

With the sunshine of an 1825 spring on his back Angus Cameron talks of retirement. As Uncle Æneas' wealthy heir, he imagines himself a gentleman farmer on Lake Lachine property bought four years ago from Alex McDougall's family.

But by July of next year, heart-stopping news of McGillivray's Thain & Company's bankruptcy shatters his farm fantasy. For this old firm of North West Company agents had held all of Æneas' money plus Angus' own savings in trust. Although the Hudson's Bay Company has already named Chief Trader Allan McDonell as Cameron's replacement, Governor Simpson takes salvage control of the ruined Montreal agency and advises Angus to postpone his retirement. Angus thankfully agrees. But he first needs time to unravel his disastrous affairs. Even the title to McDougall's farm, he has lost as the North West Company agents neglected to pay any money.

Meanwhile, on his way west, Governor Simpson in a surprise sidetrip from Mattawa to Fort Temiskaming angrily finds only clerks, newly hired George Ross and the older John McKay, in charge. McDonell, travelling overland from Lake Nipissing, has not yet arrived; Cameron has gone to Montreal. Impressed, though, by the trim efficiency of the old Fort and the prime quality of its furs, Simpson persuades Angus Cameron to stay the winter at Fort Temiskaming, in joint control with Allan McDonell. As the Montreal court, however, investigating Cameron's legal entanglement,orders Angus to remain close by in Lower Canada, Governor Simpson must transfer him as chief trader to the Lake of Two Mountains district.

Now Governor of the Southern Department, Simpson wants to end what he considers too expensive a reliance on supplies from Montreal. If anything, he believes, the Montreal office should confine its expertise to keeping opposition Canadian traders off the Ottawa River, away from Temiskaming district. What he most wants to end, though, is the central dominance of Fort Temiskaming, especially the Temiskaming Indians' heartfelt sense of loyalty to its oldtime Montreal ways. Stop this love affair and establish Moose Factory's rational Hudson's Bay Company rule over Temiskaming, Simpson urges. First, Fort Abitibi should receive its supplies of seventy pieces from the Moose district next spring. By 1829, Simpson dictates, the other Temiskaming posts should receive their 250 pieces from a Lake Superior depot. The Temiskaming Indians would pick up these pieces at Lake Nipissing for the old Fort and Grand Lac posts. Outposts such as Matawagamingue and Flying Post will depend on other Lake Superior routes.

Simpson does foresee a problem, though. If the Temiskaming Indians have to pick up distant supplies in the south, how many canoeists will remain to deliver furs to the Bay? Nevertheless, with four fur-laden canoes manned by twenty-three Indians, many of them only boys, McDonell leaves the old Fort in June, 1830, for Moose Factory. He fidgets several days at Fort Abitibi, waiting for George Bryson's canoes from Grand Lac and Trout Lake. By June 10, though, afraid his inexperienced, homesick canoemen will desert, he carries on for the Moose. Blaming his delay on his own lack of skilled paddlers, Bryson arrives three days later. What he most blames, however, is the Hudson's Bay Company's forcing him to leave his understaffed Trout Lake outpost easy prey for petty traders: only an old man remains there. McPherson is also weakly alone at Grand Lac. McDonell has left only two men at Fort Temiskaming. And even though Chief Factor John George McTavish feasts the novice Indian paddlers at Moose Factory, many of them vow not to give up next summer's rest time with their families; if we must deliver our own furs from now on, why not take advantage of a shorter, easier trip to the petty traders of Mattawa or Lake Nipissing? they whisper to one another. Yet additional wages will persuade most of them to stay paddling for the Hudson's Bay Company next year. How many more times, though, before a higher bidder appears?

Even Governor Simpson now admits the Temiskaming Indians continued loyalty to old Canadian habits is less of a threat to Hudson's Bay Company profits than the competition from more and more petty traders moving into Temiskaming from Upper Canada. And, maybe now, loyalty will prove the Company's best defence.

The most persistent Upper Canada free trading annoyance is moving in southwest from Penetanguishene. Andrew Mitchell, a fur merchant there, supplies most of the Lake Huron traders and arranges his village's annual fur auction. Two of his Penetanguishene acquaintances, Samuel Peck and Charles Harris, during the 1833-34 winter, shift their post up the Sturgeon River from Lake Nipissing to Lake Temagamang. Only twelve years ago, Angus Cameron warned Joseph Beioley of the American Fur Company's brief intrusion there. Today with more brazen traders scavenging this seldom visited lake country for loose Indian furs, Fort Temiskaming, the closest of all the Hudson's Bay Company posts, must somehow chase them away. So in defence of this upper Matabitchuan country, Angus Cameron, who inspires much Indian loyalty, returns.

6

Cabin Logs With Bark Still Rough

After Angus Cameron takes over, September, 1834, control of Fort Temiskaming, he soon discovers his predecessor, Allan McDonell, although ailing, has persuaded Penetanguishene trader Charles Harris to join the Hudson's Bay Company. And back forty miles to warm a winter outpost on the small, south shore cove of Temagami Island, he has sent Harris. Throughout the winter further south on Lake Nipissing, Richard Hardisty's Canadian helpers dog the other Penetanguishene fugitive Samuel Peck's every move. Finally in disgust Peck runs the French River down to Georgian Bay and the privacy of home.

To strengthen Cameron's bid to fence off the Temiskaming district from other Upper Canadians sneaking in from the southwest, Governor Simpson transfers Lake Nipissing's Sturgeon Hall post from Lake Huron district to Fort Temiskaming's control. And to block lumbermen from the southeast direction of Hull, fur trading their tree stump way up the Ottawa River, he also transfers Fort Coulonge's Mattawa Post. But not much of a fortress is the Mattawa storehouse, as rival shantymen sneer over the counter at its paltry pile of trade good weapons. Nevertheless, against all mercenary invaders, Angus Cameron can now co-ordinate resistance.

But what about selfless newcomers like church missionaries in search of souls? No problem, Cameron replies, so long as they do not meddle between Indian hunter and Hudson's Bay Company buyer. On July 16, 1836, the Montreal Sulpician Louis-Charles de Bellefeuille and secular priest Jean-Baptiste Dupuy knock on his door at Fort Temiskaming. After having their trunk and bags carried to an upstairs room, Angus dines them that evening. The local Indians, however, terrified these black gowned medicine men have landed to steal their spirits, stampede into the bush. Next morning, old man Cartier, once a voyageur, now enjoying his ninety-six Roman Catholic years at peace among old Fort memories, reassures the priests of the Indians' gentle hospitality. And yes, within two days, curious canoe loads of men and women slide back to their campsites. By week's end, Father Bellefeuille, north of Angus Cameron's house above the Narrows' beach encampment, has set up a large log cross beside the Company's old storage shed within which he says his first Mass.

Yet when the priests later chat of having visited George McConnell's lumber depot at Seven League Lake above Mattawa, Angus Cameron irreverently bristles. With his seven sons from Hull the American McConnell will soon spy the timber wealth crowding Lake Temiskaming. Also among these trees he will find crawling-bonus fur profits. Pity the poor Indian trappers? Rather pity the Hudson's Bay Company business, Cameron mutters. But into the conversation rings the clear eager voice of James Cameron, Angus' young nephew whom he brought back from Scotland for a training summer at the Fort before moving him on to Flying Post in September. To outsmart the gathering invasion of petty traders Temiskaming will need strong commanders.

Next May, Governor Simpson writes of a new defensive strategy to make the lake less attractive to lumbermen: buy the first large island north of the Narrows and axe down its valuable pine. How to discourage McConnell's extra interest in money-making furs? In August, Cameron meets with Simpson at Mattawa where they select a better site for a larger trading store, one well stocked enough to outbid all comers. On the north side point of land where the Mattawa River mouth touches the Ottawa, they hammer location stakes. On September 9, woodchips fly as Nicolas Brown from Fort des Allumettes starts fitting the log walls. Frances Simpson, the Governor's wife, describes Brown as "a curious dapper little man, Irish by his accent full of drollery and as busy as a bee." He will weather the winter here ready for hand-to-hand trading in the spring. And even before, as some of his men in the deepest snows backpacking their trade goods into the bush seek out Indian lodges and prime furs. Give the shantymen no head start, they say.

Starting up Lake Temiskaming on his further way to Moose Factory one golden September day, Simpson shares Cameron's canoe. Their small brigade slows at Opemican Narrows where they size up the tall grass waving around the west shore creek mouth. What a place for a farm! Wait till the lumbermen see this! Useless it is for us to dream of co-existence with the lumbermen, Simpson groans: by using our Indians, McConnell reduces the numbers hunting fur, and by paying them higher wages than they can earn selling fur, he destroys their desire to return to the hunt. By his paying the remaining hunters cash for their furs, how long before these Indians turn their noses up at our Company trade goods? Of the shantyman's flowing use of liquor to float free Indian furs, both men shake their heads. Even though

Upper Canada has just outlawed these liquor sales, how can it police such a vast wilderness?

From Fort Temiskaming, Angus Cameron takes Simpson on tour of Indian pasture lands and New Farm at the Head of the Lake. Without hay, he argues, the lumbermen will have no horses strong enough to haul timber. So without these naturally lush fields, the main source of $5.00 a ton hay on this upper lake, the McConnell's will have to pay an impossible price for imported feed. Simpson agrees the Hudson's Bay Company must control all this land. In the meantime, because the mounting competition is driving up local fur prices, he promises to supply Cameron with many more trade goods: next year after their delivery of furs to Moose Factory the canoes will bring back 180 extra pieces for Grand Lac and Fort Temiskaming; another 300 pieces will come directly from Montreal; Lake Huron district can supply Nipissing outpost.

In late October, word sighs back from Montreal that Father Bellefeuille has died of typhus. Tenting this past summer among the Indians around Lake Temiskaming, travelling as far as Lake Abitibi and Grand Lac, he never once, Angus Cameron says, interfered with our trading ways.

And next summer Cameron speaks much the same of Bellefeuille's replacement from Quebec diocese. With missionary zeal, Father Poiré first scrounges cedar posts, logs and planking for a small chapel beside last year's rusty tool shed church above the Narrows. And close by, a smaller parsonage also rises. With this convenient foothold he can stretch his mission field out to the Ottawa River headwaters of Trout Lake. Landing back at Fort Temiskaming in early September, he then reveals his grandest ambition of seeing James Bay by 1840. Perhaps, though, Angus Cameron murmurs to his nephew James passing by to his latest posting at Temagami, this is going too far, too soon.

For the Protestant clergy at York Factory claim the Hudson's Bay territory as their own. Governor Simpson, already angered elsewhere at Red River by Roman Catholic missionary Father Belcourt's support of the rebellious Métis against Hudson's Bay Company rule will certainly object. And he soon does, as early in 1839 he asks the London Committee to have the more pliable Wesleyan Society send sufficient missionaries to fill all Christian needs on the Bay.

But as if Roman Catholic ambitions were a warning of other headaches to follow, the McConnells suddenly make their move to Lake Temiskaming and build a lumbering depot at Opemican Creek with timber berths all the way north to Matabitchuan River.

Returning next spring from a furlough in Scotland and cheered by his new title of Chief Factor, Angus Cameron soon sours. Thomas Fraser and Fort Temiskaming's newest clerk, Governor Simpson's brother-in-law John Simpson, tell him of McConnell's many men defiantly poaching local furs.

Then in June, George McConnell bellows from a northbound boat he has as much right to Lake Temiskaming haylands as anyone else. Now convinced the only way to rid the district of McConnell and his sons is to beat them at their own lumbering game, Cameron pays Bytown's standard $1.00 per square mile timber licence fee for the rest of the lake's two mile depth of cutting limits and haylands from Matabitchuan River north to the Head of the Lake. With oxen and horses driven in through the bush from Mattawa, he then hires master William Armstrong to outfit three shanties up the western shore.

Over the 1840 summer, Cameron loses more sleep foiling the Roman Catholic advance on Hudson Bay. On his April return from London he brought the Wesleyan minister George Barnley who quickly nagged his impatient way up lakes Temiskaming and Abitibi to missionary room and board at Moose Factory. As soon as Father Poiré's threatening summer rounds bend north to Fort Abitibi, Thomas Fraser politely tells him of Barnley's recent stopover and how his own obedient Hudson's Bay preference is for local Indians to follow the Protestant faith. No insults but neither friendly encouragement. Left talking to himself, Poiré retreats south.

Seven days later, he hails eighteen-year-old Eppie (Elizabeth) Cameron in her lone canoe exploring Lake Temiskaming's northern bowl of clay brown water, seemingly held by the limestone handle of Wabikijik Point. She has thrilled at earlier summer trips with Uncle Angus, inspecting trees along the Montreal River and farther up the western shore past the Narrows to the rounded bay where a broad, sand toasted beach between a muddy creek and rocky, right hand point faces white capped waves dancing down from the far away, pale blue line of northern lakeshore. Affectionately nicknamed ''the lady of the lake'', Eppie is looking forward to next summer's vacation from her Montreal school and a promised trip to brother James' latest posting at Grand Lac. And more so, now her cousin, twenty year old Charles Stuart, fresh from Scotland, whom Angus hired as a labourer three months ago, will also be there working for James. No one blames her for boasting of Fort Temiskaming as the Grant-Cameron-Stuart, Canadian estate. And since school studies tell her next year's government at Kingston will pass the Act of Union joining together Temiskaming's Upper and Lower Canada parts into one Province of Canada, she feels even closer to this mysterious brooding Ottawa River country.

In a chillier October, William Armstrong finishes cruising the Hudson's Bay Company timber limits for tall white pine trees. And plenty of them there are — at least one, 150 foot tall, three to four foot diameter pine for every ten smaller ones, each worth $200.00 at Quebec for ship masts in England. Impossible to miss, their giant trunks soar knot clean of branches for the first seventy feet. He finally spots his shanty sites close enough to river or stream for easy haulage among these outstanding timbers.

In December, the head swamper's gang clears winter roads up the simplest grades through ravines or along small creek beds. Then, at the river bank near each Pinery site they take half a week to build a stable for ten pair of horses, a small storehouse, a granary and low roofed shanty large enough for fifty men. Made out of sixteen-inch-diameter notched logs the forty by thirty foot long shanty's eight foot high walls rise. Not of poplar logs, though; superstition whispers they bring accidents and sickness. Hollowed out scoops of log, sloped just enough to run the water off, cover the roof. A separate set of these overlapping concave logs reaches up from the top of each side wall halfway across to rest on one of a pair of solid pine beams spanning the building's length. Sealing the ridge crack where the two roof sets peak is a single line of trough logs concave side down.

Through the five foot square door, in the middle of the adzed timber floor sits a twelve foot square fireplace, the camboose, walled in by twelve by twelve inch hardwood timbers and filled with sand a foot deep. One corner with its own twenty inch hardwood square next to the cook's table is for cooking beans or meat in hot sand. At the pole edge of this "Bean Hole", a crane swings iron kettles out over the fire in the camboose centre. A hole of equal camboose size in the roof above with a four foot high wooden smokestack tapering to a four foot square provides ventilation and light. For only two small windows front and rear break the shanty walls. Supported four feet above the roof hole an open belfry keeps the snow out. Be quick when opening the shanty door: thick smoke from its sudden draught could billow back down the chimney throughout the room.

Rough poles frame double beds two tiers high. Cushioned with balsam boughs or loose straw these bunks stand six feet out from one side wall and the end wall opposite the door. Squared timbers balanced on blocks provide a single bench all around the bunk area.

Between the door and the bunk area's side wall are the wash trough and water barrels. Close to the other side of the door is the clerk's writing desk, then a short space before the cook's table at the corner. Bread troughs and ladles hang on the wall. Off limits to other shantymen, down the other side wall are the cook, clerk and foreman's double beds. The cook's helper, his "devil", sleeps on the other side with the men. Governor Simpson has reminded Angus Cameron to make sure the clerk sells Company dry goods, especially the ready made clothing from Fort Temiskaming's storehouse. Compared to McConnell's camps, the Hudson's Bay Company shanties spill over with barrel supplies for men and animals.

Meal time? Ladle pork and beans, pea soup, molasses on to your tin plate. Sit on the bench, soak the food up with your bread or spoon it down. Boiled for an hour "tea soup" splashes from the swinging kettle into your bowl and down your scorched throat. A Sunday treat cheers the routine when cook ladles out the "sea pie" of left over pork, beef, bread dough and lard baked in the iron kettle overnight. Then after washing sweat stained flannel shirts and patching grey cloth trousers you can put up your cowhide boots with heavy spikes for the rest of the day.

Camboose Cook (Picturesque Canada)

Around the half-a-cord-a-day camboose flames, story telling, singing, fiddle or mouth organ music pass Saturday evening hours. But weeknights are for sharpening tomorrow's axes. And with a week's supply for only a nickel, clay pipefuls of Canadian Twist cloud the air. Soon, still clothed with stockinged feet toward the fire and two men to a blanket bed, the whole crew snores. Up for 5:00 o'clock breakfast, the same food as supper. Out into the winter darkness with axe and lunchpail for 6:00 o'clock work. Only the flambeau rope dipped in tallow lights their dark, knee deep trail.

Three lumberjacks fell a tree, square its twelve inch butt, then leave it for two sawyers to chop the trunk into forty-or fifty-foot lengths, square all ends and cant hook the sticks into position so scorers and razor sharp broad axes can finish the shaping job. Skidding crews then hammer the company brand on, hitch oxen to the timbers which hauled out to the road neatly pile up on skids for stronger horse teams to drag over hard packed snow to the river's edge and a spring roll.

Six pieces of timber or about 400 cubic feet a day each crew cuts, squares and piles. A penny tax for each cubic foot the Hudson's Bay Company must pay the government but each stick sells for $20.00 at Quebec. About the shantyman's wage of $15.00 a month plus free room and board, Governor Simpson does grumble; yet, he admits, it is a price worth paying to destroy McConnell's Temiskaming lumber-fur trade hopes.

So hard working are Cameron's 1840-41 winter crews in opposition to all other shanties, the McConnells offer to quit Lake Temiskaming if the Hudson's Bay Company will buy their entire stock. Having had no free winter time to make money trading for furs and now with the lake level so low no one can float lumber out of Lake Temiskaming, they have no other choice. Over Cameron's best price the seven brothers haggle, however. And after Governor Simpson realizes if he pays them too much, other lumbermen will blackmail him into a similar deal, he advises Angus Cameron to continue their war against the McConnells. Cameron's 1841-42 licence claims the same limits with an additional mile of depth up the western shore. And more, he can cut thirty thousand feet of red pine not only on the west side of the lake but also on the east from a point opposite the Montreal River mouth up to the foot of the large island north of the old Fort Narrows.

What though, in the meantime, of the more delicate Hudson's Bay Company manoeuverings against Father Poiré who still insists on journeying to Moose Factory? Thomas Fraser at Fort Abitibi reads Governor Simpson's 1841 letter warning him to "exert your ingenuity to keep Guides and Interpreters out of his way and to prevent his employing the Indians in erecting buildings, voyaging, taking supplies, or any other way that is likely to operate our desire of extending the Protestant Religion among the Tribes." So, again, beyond Abitibi Father Poiré cannot go. But after he files his winter report of Fraser's refusal to let him even build an Abitibi chapel, the Bishop of Quebec threatens an appeal to the British Parliament. The Hudson's Bay Company immediately pleads any Roman Catholic opposition to the Protestant mission on the Bay will confuse the Indians and risk losing their Christianity altogether. As to the Bishop's second complaint Thomas Fraser was bribing the Indians with liquor, the Company suggests petty fur traders in the area forced Fraser recently into a practice he otherwise abhors; or maybe other Indian voyageurs on their spring brigade way to the Moose bullied Fraser into uncorking the bottle.

By September of next year the stubborn McConnells are threatening their own push further north to the Head of Lake Temiskaming. And fatalistic they are: any lumber money they lose, furs will make up. But hoping to bankrupt them once and for all this coming 1842-43 winter, Angus Cameron has permission to cut three miles farther up Quinze River from the Head of the Lake fifteen thousand feet of the best red pine. Is he wasting his Company's competitive fur trade time, though? For now while the Company's back is turned the notorious free traders McGillivray and Day have crept up through the rapids from Mattawa on to Lake Temiskaming. Not lumbering people these; their one naked lust is fur. One pirate swipe, when they offer to triple the annual salary of one of Cameron's best clerks in return for precise information on the most productive fur areas, disgusts Angus Cameron. So just as soon as the McConnells in February abandon their bankrupted shanties between Mattawa and Fort Temiskaming, Angus Cameron quits cutting timber to focus full attention on crushing McGillivray and Day. Yet to his dismay, as the McConnells herd their horses and lumbering tools south to their Deep River farm they leave men behind to go after Indian furs, so doubling the Hudson's Bay Company surveillance work.

Yet not even this disappointment can spoil Angus Cameron's smiling retirement plans. He may have missed the opportunity seventeen years ago, but today, sixty-one years old, nothing can bar him from quiet rest and family life.

To help Angus' replacement, Thomas Fraser, handle the violent trade on Lake Temiskaming, Governor Simpson sends extra supplies and more men in the June canoes. Give the Indian traders whatever they want, he says, and have the new men match opposition fur traders, footstep-for-footstep.

But too little time is there to sing Angus Cameron's farewell as the harried Governor also glowers at this summer's Roman Catholic missionaries. Without warning, Father Moreau, Poiré's replacement, has arrived at Fort Temiskaming with two Oblate priests on tour of their order's new mission field. Alarmed at their rumoured plan for a permanent mission house on the Height of Land, Akokwehidjiwan as the Lake Abitibi Indians still call it. Simpson knows these Indians from the north, attracted to such a house, would fall easy prey to any petty traders prowling the southern slopes. So to protect local Indian furs for himself, Governor Simpson finally lets the Roman Catholics build their summer chapel beside Fort Abitibi. That Father Moreau soon after refuses the McConnells' offer to weatherproof his Fort Temiskaming chapel, if he will bless their good trade behaviour in front of the local Indians, is hopeful evidence, Simpson believes, of future Roman Catholic honesty.

While visiting Fort Temiskaming in October, Simpson senses Thomas Fraser's unhappiness. Never hardened by low-blow experiences similar to Angus Cameron's Matawagamingue days, he cannot cope with Temiskaming's unrelenting battle of fur trade wits. So Chief Trader John

Siveright of Fort Coulonge takes charge of the district and back north Fraser joyfully skips. With a half smile, though, after Simpson tells him to break his company's recent promise to help construct a temporary Roman Catholic mission on Lake Abitibi.

On not only his own but anyone's word Simpson places cynical value. Seated soon after at the small table in the front hall room of Fort Temiskaming House he listens to Rinaldo and Benjamin McConnell promise to stop all fur trading if the Hudson's Bay Company will loan them £500 for a return to their Lake Temiskaming lumber business. Can he trust them? He surely wants to and he advises John Siveright if they should later present a more secure promise, take it; in the meantime, however, with the highest fur prices we can afford, squeeze the living trade out of them.

TABLES shewing the Monthly Mean Temperature (Farnh. Therm.) for two years, at the Hudson Bay Company's Post on Lake Temiscaming, Lat. 47° 19′ North ; Long. 79° 31′ West ; 630 feet above the level of the sea.—From a Register kept by Mr. Severight.

1843-4.

MONTH.	Sunrise.	Noon.	Sunset.	Mean for each month.	Clear sunshine.	Clear and cloudy.	Cloudy.	Cloudy and rain.	Cloudy and snow.
1843.									
November	24 5/30	29 6/30	27	26 2/3	3	10	5	2	10
December	18 26/31	26 5/31	22 25/31	22 1/2	2	10	13	1	5
1844.									
January	−1 12/31	12 24/31	10 2/31	7 1/6	13	5	6	....	7
February	8 24/29	28 6/29	19 22/29	19	7	9	6	....	7
March	13 18/31	33	25 10/31	23 1/3	14	8	5	....	4
April	33 17/30	53 23/30	45 2/30	44	23	1	2	4	....
May	42 4/31	57 14/31	50 14/31	50	12	8	....	11	....
June	56 2/30	70 22/30	61 6/30	62 2/3	11	4	3	12	....
July	58 5/31	72 11/31	66 15/31	65 2/3	9	8	3	11	....
August	56 26/31	71 9/31	63 25/31	64	10	6	....	15	....
September	48	63 15/30	56 15/30	56	13	7	1	9	....
October	34 6/31	46	42 9/31	40 5/6	11	8	1	5	6

1844-5.

MONTH.	Sunrise.	Noon.	Sunset.	Mean for each month.	Clear sunshine.	Clear and cloudy.	Cloudy.	Cloudy and rain.	Cloudy and snow.
1844.									
November	24 16/30	31 4/30	28 4/30	28	4	7	8	3	8
December	11 23/31	19 14/31	16 8/31	15 5/6	9	8	8	....	6
1845.									
January	8 19/31	17 23/31	13 18/31	13 1/3	6	15	3	1	6
February	11 15/28	24 25/28	20 4/28	18 5/6	7	8	5	3	5
March	19	34 25/31	28 20/31	27 1/2	9	10	3	2	7
April	26 19/31	43 16/30	36	35 1/3	5	11	....	8	6
May	38 16/31	56	49	47 5/6	13	7	5	6	....
June	51 18/30	69 25/30	62 6/30	61 1/6	12	7	5	6	....
July	58	75 7/31	67 27/31	67	8	12	....	11	....
August	58	76 16/31	67 9/31	67 1/3	15	10	....	6	....
September	48 7/30	58 5/30	53 14/30	53 1/3	1	8	2	19	....
October	38	50	46	44 2/3	11	10	3	7	....

Though short of fur trade breath in the summer of 1844, and without any Hudson's Bay Company money, the McConnells still move their shantymen back. And they are also vowing to pick more furs out of Indian hands. At this same agitating time, thirty year old Oblate Father Nicholas Laverlochère arrives to build Abitibi mission. Only a temporary one, though, Governor Simpson scolds.

Next summer Simpson hires Albert Wilmot of Allumettes Island who three years ago had rafted Angus Cameron's timber to Quebec. By sharing profits with this cost-conscious lumberman, the Hudson's Bay Company will not only cover its expenses but will also use his shantymen to scare away opposition fur grabbers. Yet as Cameron's poorly squared sticks took such a long, credit-wracking time to sell, a risky business this is. And what if shanty costs exceed the falling market price for timber? But when Wilmot, in readying his June, 1848, start, discovers John Egan and Company holds, except for the Blanche River area, all the land around Lake Temiskaming, any risk ends. And even if some lumbering road could be found through the Blanche's tangle of deadfalls, too small are its trees. With no choice but to cancel Wilmot's contract and write off the extra shanty supplies, Governor Simpson appears to have lost the latest McConnell battle.

Nevertheless, perseverance and luck combine: in a chance July conversation John Egan promises Simpson none of his contractors, McConnells included, will interfere with the Hudson's Bay Company fur trade. Furthermore, Egan does not want any of his highly paid shantymen cheating company time by running after Indian furs. So after ten splintering years, Fort Temiskaming may still have its shanty neighbours but it can finally look forward to them minding their own business.

No wonder John Egan can afford neutrality. Along the Ottawa his gigantic operation uses 1,700 horses, 200 bullocks and 400 double teams on the road for hauling food and forage. He has 100 shanties, employs 3,800 men who consume 1000 barrels of pork each year. His total operation costs $2,000,000 annually.

Still a bother, though, are the Roman Catholic missionaries. By 1846 with a growing congregation at Abitibi, Fathers Laverlochère and Clément are preaching of the need for more converts from Hudson Bay. And next year in July, with six Canadian paddlers and an Indian to guide them, Laverlochère and his new assistant Father Guerin follow the annual fur brigade from Abitibi down to Moose Factory. Once there, they insist the outpost Indians are begging them for a year round mission. Yet Simpson warns any permanent mission will cause the Indians to settle near the church, forget their self sufficient nomadic skills and starve. Chief Factor Robert Miles, however, personally enjoys the priests' open-hearted answers; not so the Wesleyan George Barnley who is so furious he clambers aboard the autumn ship for England.

Perhaps the terrifying scourge of last year may have blackened Barnley's latest mood. Desert dry from a searing sun, Temiskaming's forests burned all last summer. Most of the timber and fur bearing animals, especially around Lake Temagami, flamed into smouldering waste. A sick Alexander McDonnell, faced with starvation, had left his Temagami outpost during the previous winter and then refused to return in the summer heat. Every week, whole Indian families died from tuberculosis not only at Temagami but throughout the district. With fewer Indian hunters, today's fur trade could collapse. And the threat of tuberculosis, which continues to kill, could possibly have chased Barnley away from Hudson Bay.

When John Siveright finally achieves chief factor pension status in 1846 he retires out of the way of James Cameron who a year later, although still only a clerk, succeeds as chief of Temiskaming district. And James' cousin, Charles Stuart, though only a postmaster, succeeds him at Grand Lac. Then his sister Eppie marries widower John George McTavish whom she first met five years earlier at the Lake of Two Mountains district where he is still chief factor.

James Cameron inherits an emerging Temiskaming problem—the scarcity of people willing or able to work for the Hudson's Bay Company. Other countries are now attracting most of Britain's emigrants while other jobs closer to town or city captivate Canada's youth. To make best use of fewer skilled servants of the Company, Cameron merges the small Temiskaming outposts on Opemika Creek and Lake Kipewa into a more central post—James Hunter's Lodge on a far eastern arm of Lake Kipewa. And unable to find by the summer of 1848 a clerk or postmaster for the still vacant Temagami post, Cameron places the unranked Canadian Moïse Lavallée there. Besides this shortage of qualified staff, James Cameron fears Indian hunters, already spoiled by cash payments from petty traders, are growing much too independent while idled by tranquil church village life.

With a Hudson's Bay Company sloop carrying his mission even farther north this 1848 summer, Father Laverlochère meets the Indians of Fort Albany. Though he still has no permanent mission base, his visits throughout Temiskaming do stir Indian thoughts of a life devoted to Christ, not the Hudson's Bay Company. Yet his faith is not the only revolutionary influence in Temiskaming.

For the Hudson's Bay Company itself, farther south down the Ottawa River, is spending more and more time dealing with lumbermen's retail needs than the traditional business of trading for furs with the Indians. For this reason James Cameron resents the transfer of Mattawa Post to Hector McKenzie's more liberal Lac des Allumettes district, now reduced to a post office called Fort William. But so eager are the crowded lumbermen at this lower reach of the Ottawa to spend money, McKenzie would be a fool to refuse taking it. Small wonder he expects Colin Rankin at the upriver Mattawa Post to follow his profitable lead into the provision store business.

James Cameron worries, though: how much longer can the Temiskaming Indian-Hudson's Bay Company fur trade marriage last if such alienation is allowed to creep up to Lake Temiskaming?

Ojibway Indian Chief and Wife

During the 1849 mild spell of January's final day, Thomas Fraser dies. Again placed in temporary charge, William Paulson chooses Fraser's Indian friends to bear his coffin to Fort Abitibi's frost-deep graveyard. But no one expects the year's next blow, when one soft September afternoon James Cameron, now a confident, thirty-two year old chief trader, topples to the floor of his Fort Temiskaming porch, blood gushing from a bullet wound in the neck. King, the English clerk, horseplaying with an old gun accidentally triggered it. And after James McKay, Donald's grandson, stops the bleeding, he can only help cradle the limp body to an upstairs room. Hector McKenzie arrives within a week and when he finds James Cameron still chalk white from loss of blood he has him gently placed in the bottom of a canoe for a quick trip to hospital in Montreal. Yet by January he is surprisingly well enough to ride a dog sled back.

Now sure of Cameron's recovery, Governor Simpson returns his Temiskaming time to the annual frustration of Roman Catholic missionaries. Since the Wesleyan Society has refused to replace George Barnley, the Church of England now recognizes Rupert's Land as a diocese and sends James Horden to Moose Factory. And Simpson can refuse Father Laverlochère's latest rival plea for permanent missions at Abitibi and Moose. But so long as he does not upset Protestant congregations, Laverlochère may build another temporary one at Fort Albany; but only for summer use, Simpson reminds him.

By October, alarmed by James Cameron's deteriorating health, Simpson orders Hector McKenzie to relieve him again at the old Fort. And devastated by dizzy spells Cameron staggers his leave of absence way to Scotland. Oddly reminiscent of James' youthful start fourteen years ago, Simpson sends Robert Hamilton to Abitibi where William Paulson will train him as a clerk, minimum requirements for the late Thomas Fraser's position. Then within four months, as James Cameron also drops dead, Hector McKenzie must take his place.

Because in the lumber country below Mattawa, fur trading has scattered out of Hudson's Bay Company control, Governor Simpson decides to combine Temiskaming and Lac des Allumettes districts under the supervision of McKenzie who will continue to live at his Fort William home, while John Simpson, now chief Trader at Lake Nipissing, will take resident charge of the Fort Temiskaming post.

Yet by that 1851 summer day when John Simpson sees Father Laverlochère's limp body in the bottom of a canoe racing through the old Fort Narrows on its way to Montreal, he wonders if the land is cursed. Just a year ago was James Cameron shot and now Father Laverlochère, only thirty-six years old, looks as if he is dying. On his portage way to Moose Factory after walking around Couchiching Falls, Iroquois Falls, the Long Sault rapids, the Three Carrying Places, the Lopstick Portage and finally the Long Portage around the solid rock gorge of Abitibi River he collapsed. While lugging his share of baggage up the steep 200 foot canyon slope, footsteps above a sheer 100 foot cliff spur crazily bulging out over the river edge below, he slumped paralyzed on to the trail.

Maybe, though, Hector McKenzie's August 15 wedding can lift the gloom. That his bride, Mary Ballantyne is the daughter of Sir Walter Scott's publisher and sister of the former Hudson's Bay Company clerk, Robert Ballantyne, now the popular author of Hudson Bay stories, restores a sense of romantic adventure. Even though more and more shanties cut larger holes into Lake Temiskaming's surrounding bush and reveal the many hiding places of petty traders, the old Company, at least, might still have the unyielding strength of an ancient Ulysses.

Since Hector McKenzie prefers prolonging his 1852 honeymoon bliss at Fort William, John Simpson, busier at the Fort Temiskaming fur trade location, takes sole command of the two districts. Distant news, though, warns him more people may soon be travelling north to slow business down. The Ontario, Simcoe and Huron Railway in Canada West nears October completion. As soon as snowdrifts melt next April, the *Lady Elgin* locomotive, lamp black and elegant in brass fittings, will belch cinders along its maiden run from Toronto north to Machell's Corners. Already the Bytown and Prescott line connects, on the American side of the St. Lawrence River at Ogdensburg, with a network spreading south into New England. Along these railway tracks travel most of today's sawlogs from Ottawa River shanties.

What of Canadian square timber profits? For the last ten years duty-free Russian Baltic timber has supplied most of Britain's need. In the meantime, though, as New England's saw mills have exhausted their own country's forest reserves, American lumbermen have explored north. Fifty years ago Philemon Wright of Massachusetts came in search of square timber, but now other lumber merchants like Ezra Bronson and J.H. Harris from New York State, C.A. Pattie and William Perley from New Hampshire, are investing fortunes in Canadian bush camps and saw mills. Even twenty-six year old Ezra Butler Eddy from Bristol, Vermont has a small match stick factory in Hull. And since he is changing from spark spitting "lucifers" to the new phosphorous-tipped safety matches, the factory, they say, might grow larger.

Selling shanty supplies in the middle of this saw log boom, Hector McKenzie's store continues thriving. A few furs cross his counter but only a few remain in the surrounding bush. As the Americans are steadily working north in search of more red and white pine trees for their mills, John Simpson, like James Cameron four years ago, fears Fort Temiskaming will soon be reduced to the same servile store business as Fort Coulonge.

And when the 1854 Reciprocity Treaty between the British North American provinces and the United States, gives Canadian lumber free passage to American markets, no one disagrees with him. This summer, though, still in advance of the saw mill Americans, Gilmour and Egan's square timbering shanties surround Lake Temiskaming - Gilmour on the west, Egan on the east. Rinaldo McConnell and his foreman Baptiste Jolicoeur prosper with their Opemika operation. Donald Cameron with his shanty at the north end of Lake Kipewa also has a farm there just fifteen miles to the southeast of Fort Temiskaming. To bring in hay from the Head of Lake Temiskaming, Cameron has built a winter road from Big Stone River, two miles below the old Fort, over to his Kipewa shanty. And on the side, he too trades for furs. Still a lucrative business here, as two former lumberjacks who spend all their time trapping at Lake Kipewa also know. As usual the Hudson's Bay Company grinds its corporate teeth.

Always worried about costs eating into Company profits and weakening its competitive edge, Governor Simpson is seeking a solution to the expensive transport of Montreal supplies to Fort Temiskaming and Abitibi. Canoes or winter transport? Horses with double sleighs each bearing loads of 1,800 pounds from Montreal up the Ottawa River ice to Mattawa depot win out. Spring canoes from lakes Temiskaming and Abitibi can run the rapids to pick up these supplies for the rest of the trip north. Yet two years from now Governor Simpson will cancel winter transport and once again rely on canoes for the whole trip. From Lachine he will then write, "We shall send from hence at the opening of the navigation 2 large canoes manned by 16 Iroquois Goers and Comers engaged to make as many trips as may be required between the Joachim and Temiscamingue, 5 or 6 will probably be sufficient; - they will take as cargo from this place about 50 pieces in each canoe, consisting of grease, pork, tobacco & sundries...." Three years later, however, Simpson will change his mind back again to winter transport.

Even before this last change, though, the June, 1855, Indian paddlers arriving at Fort Temiskaming with the Montreal goods think the Hudson's Bay Company must be saving money if it can afford to build the new board fence enclosing the warehouse and dwellings. A tall spiked arch now crowns the twin-doored gate centered in the wide run of whitewashed palings set between front yard and beach. Inside the gate, beside the old store and in front of John Simpson's house, is the oak tree of Saint-Louis that Father Poiré planted seventeen years ago in thanks for his first chapel. Simpson's three storey, whitewashed timber house has a new shingle roof with three third-floor dormers facing the sun; two others pierce the back roof. To make one large reception room for himself, Simpson has taken out the wall between the kitchen and downstairs bedroom. Upstairs are a drawing room and three yellow walled bedrooms, one of them kept for Governor Simpson.

Through one of the new dormer windows is seen the flag pole soaring into the light blue sky. And sixty-four year old William Paulson (by now used to seeing his name spelled Polson), recently moved down from Fort Abitibi to help outsmart the petty traders, ambles over to the old storehouse's heavy basement door, up the steps to the open verandah along the east wall and in through a door to the fur storerooms behind the long, lattice-enclosed counter. He also has to check the rum kegs emptied this spring by Indian trappers who drank many measures as reward for their superior numbers of Made Marten. After counting the trade goods bales and kegs from Mattawa piled inside the smaller companion storehouse, Polson rides one of the other canoes bound for Abitibi to the Head of the Lake. There close by the Indians' summer encampment his wife, two sons, daughter and son-in-law, Angus McBride, are fitting out his retirement home where next year he can farm his summer and trap winter away.

The only year-round settler on Lake Temiskaming, he will not lack temporary guests. Familiar are the Indians, shantymen, crib rafters, and faces of Fort Temiskaming friends planting crops at New Farm or travelling on to Abitibi and Grand Lac.

One late September 1857 day, though, two strangers knock on his door. James Bangs of Arnprior and his nephew John of Pakenham declare they have arrived to go into open, fur trade competition with Fort Temiskaming. Are the Polsons willing to help? Annoyed already by such brashness, Governor Simpson has had Hector McKenzie's men follow their two canoes up the Ottawa River to keep an eye on them all winter. Now this is the last straw, Simpson swears. Contradicting his long standing practice of only paying the Indians in Made Marten credits he instructs the old Fort traders to outbid any Bangs' offer with 50 cents equivalent in gold or silver coins. Yet, as soon as Hector McKenzie arrives at the Head of the Lake, he realizes how tempted William Polson's family is to guide the Bangses' to the furs of Temiskaming. So he soon persuades Governor Simpson to grant William Polson a loyalty pension of £35 a year and hire Angus McBride, whose father George commanded Fort Temiskaming thirty-five years ago, to take charge of a small outpost far away near Grand Lac.

Suffocating under McKenzie's close watch, James Bangs in April, 1858, fights back for air. He informs the customs office at Ottawa, now capital of the Province of Canada, the Hudson's Bay Company is importing English goods into the country without paying duty. Customs agent John Heaney soon scurries up to Fort Temiskaming to seize all illegal goods. Without hesitation John Simpson invites him into the storehouse to check any supplies from Moose Factory, then casually remarks, anyone who touches them will have his hand shot off. Governor Simpson and Inspector-General Alexander Galt later agree in Montreal on the future payment of taxes. In the meantime, however, puzzled Indians unable to barter for the impounded goods have sold their furs to the Bangses. And even though the Hudson's Bay Company quickly recovers, it will forever lose the important advantage of bringing goods in through Hudson Bay.

Although the Bangses did score a point they barely remain in the game. With Angus McBride safely out of the way as an extra man at Grand Lac, Charles Stuart, the clerk there, is free to spend his 1858-59 winter at Lake Temiskaming. From a log house near William Polson's Head of the Lake home, Stuart and his clerk operate Fort Resolution solely to finish breaking the Bangses' spirit. And despite Bangses' traders waylaying Indians at the mouths of all major rivers and streams, Stuart's men step in with their surplus cash deal. So demoralizing is this interference by next September the Hudson's Bay Company even hires John Bangs away from his uncle, to work with James Hunter now at Mattawa House.

Master here for the last three years, James Hunter is operating the one and a half storey, twenty-eight by forty-five foot general store located where the Mattawa River mouth's north corner puckers into a low boulder-tumbled point. Log dwellings, warehouse and stable stretch back towards the western mound of evergreen hills. Up along the point's north side calm waters lap the curve of stone-littered beach, while south the Mattawa and Ottawa rivers wrestle into a white lather. Across the Mattawa mouth within its other pointed southern corner, this summer's wigwam village scatters. From here, Indian traders come, but more and more their frail canoes barely dodge the big logs floated down river from the west. Some of the logs, having escaped from E. Varin's depot at the Boom Lake chute, come from as far away west as Lake Talon. And so many lumbermen's spiked boots tattoo steps to the store, Indian moccasins have little room to pad. Not like former days.

And for the first time in local memory no one has heard voyageur paddles thud around the Mattawa bend towards the northwest Interior. For now any trade supplies or men from Montreal travel by railway to Toronto and Collingwood for the Great Lakes' steamer to Fort William. Odd wistful canoes on their way past to Lac des Allumettes or Lachine do career down from Fort Temiskaming. Yet how can they compare to the blood beating uproar of six fathom birch bark hulks, like upside down centipedes, churning west?

Noah Timmins is quietly applauding their absence, though. Having moved his family two years ago from Aylmer to a farm eight miles downstream on the Ottawa, he passes as much of this 1859-60 winter as possible away from shanty work to trade freely among the Indian villagers on Mattawa Point. From his rival post across the river ice, James Hunter often glimpses Timmins' blanket coat tied with its red sash and his red toque disappear into another lodge, but he is kept too busy at the store to stalk after.

In June, having replaced Father Déléage as head of the Ottawa Mission, Father Jean Marie Pian answers the annual Mattawa call. After four days here he has two Indians guide him through the rapids to Lake Temiskaming. Up near the Montreal River mouth he meets Baptiste Jolicoeur and his son-in-law, Joseph Bonin from Beauharnois, taking in supplies to Rinaldo McConnell's shanty. At Fort Temiskaming, clerk Pierre Chevrètte offers to have Moïse Lavallée repair the chapel's plank roof caved in by winter snows. But from his one room log parsonage Father Pian looks across the Narrows to the gentle shoreline space and overgrown patch of vegetable garden first cleared by Angus Cameron's men thirty-six summers ago. Why not move there? Of all the temporary Roman Catholic chapels throughout Temiskaming the one here at the Narrows has been most permanent and most central. Why not rebuild a larger, more enduring church? One that can serve as a mission base to reach out to all Temiskaming peoples and the beginning trickle of Canadian settlers? And set a permanent example for James Bay to follow. By August 9, Father Pian again stands on Mattawa Point recording its first baptism ''one Antoine Thivierge, born on the seventh of the eighth month, eighteen hundred and fifty-eight, son of Antoine Thivierge and of Mani Joseph.''

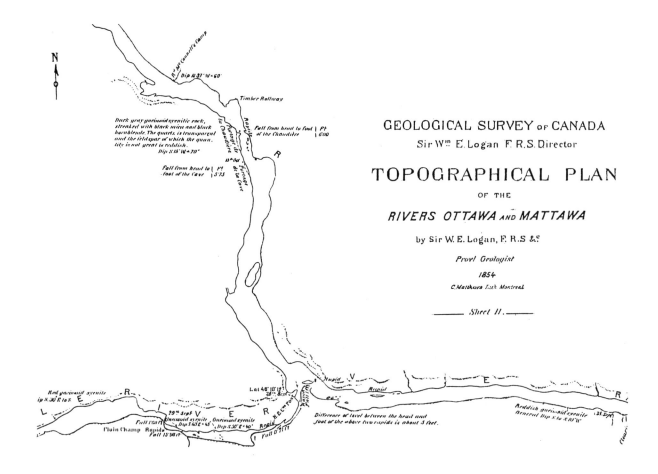

Just when such a family threatens to abandon nomadic tradings ways for a permanent place to squat, Governor George Simpson dies in September. Because he had accepted no other way of Hudson's Bay Company life than imperious feudal rule, he had never stooped low for legal title to the Company's Ottawa River lands. Yet John Siveright, even though almost deaf, grew nervous in 1845 when William Logan's geological survey of Lake Temiskaming first shouted about Canada's ownership. And two years later, government surveyors measured a right of way through Fort Coulonge ground which the Company had neglected to buy. No better than any other squatter is the Hudson's Bay Company, the surveyors said. So what is to stop any family from settling these same lands?

Should the Hudson's Bay Company expect to have more rights than any other squatter? After Rinaldo McConnell takes up the J.R. Booth Limits along Lake Temiskaming's western lakeshore north to Point à la Barbe, one mile down from the old Fort, Joseph Bonin with his wife and McConnell's camp cook, Jean Thomas Hébert, settle on the ancient Front location immediately north of the Montreal River mouth. And Baptiste Jolicoeur follows in 1861 to occupy his home offshore on the remnant fifteen acres of Montreal Island where the original Compagnie du Nord post once grandly stood. What of the equally attractive haylands at the Head of the Lake? newly appointed Chief Factor John Simpson worries. What is to stop other settlers from moving there? Next year proves this anxiety correct, when Edward Piché quits shanty life to settle his family on the eastern lakeshore opposite Wabi's Point, on another beaver meadow the Company still uses to graze its cattle. Adding insult, Piché will also trade for furs this coming winter.

With store merchants following settlers up the Ottawa River, Hector McKenzie prompts Edward Hopkins at Lachine to purchase the Company's property at Mattawa. And even though without a proper survey the description is vague, Hopkins does. Maybe none too soon, as Moïse Lavallée leaves the Hudson's Bay Company to start his own trade store below the south end of Lake Temiskaming, down river at Rapide de la Cave.

During May, 1863, Joseph Miron from Papineauville, hoping to mix shanty work and farming, settles his family a mile above Opemika Narrows on the tip of land curling around the northwest corner of McLaren's Bay. The former shantyman Meech and his Norwegian partner, who still spend most of their winter time at Lake Kipewa talking Indians out of their furs, summer camp in the same bay. Two other nomadic Norwegians annually talk their way up Matabitchuan River lakes west to Temagami.

If it were not for the thirty-two miles of violent waters above Mattawa, other families might permanently settle on Lake Temiskaming. But use this violent entry way they must; for needing summertime to build a house as well as gather food, they cannot merely wait for the easier winter ice road in. So, fearless courage it takes to unlock this hard door north. Four miles up the quarter-mile-wide Ottawa River from Mattawa lurk the Cave rapids, a half mile series of pot hole eddies. Only the most skilled canoers from its Chaudière beginning dare shoot its mad ten foot drop. Three and a half miles farther jeers the thirteen foot fall of Les Érables and its portage through half a mile of hard maple bush. The next obstacle, another three and a half miles away, is Mountain Rapids where rocks, reefs and islets fill a narrow channel between 500 foot hills. Then skimming seventeen miles against the current's constant tug, the waters of Seven League Lake lead past Old Woman Rock gnarled beside the river's edge, past the sheer east side precipice of Devil's Garden where wild onions mysteriously grow, and past thickly overgrown La Tuque hill whose small pine trees sharply butt into the western sky. Suddenly the last dragon length of six, lashing Long Sault miles, with some of its massive boulders twelve to fifteen feet in diameter, terrorize the settler's last breath: pulling boats through shoulder deep water sluicing over slime greased boulders along the western shore, portaging east around bottomless Red Pine Eddy, around the rock cut into Crooked Rapid, then around Flat Rapid until you stagger up the west side bush trail finally to collapse on Lake Temiskaming's shore.

After three years of Long Sault staggers, Father Pian feels he deserves good settlement fortune. And since Bishop Bourget has blessed the purchase of ninety-five acres opposite Fort Temiskaming, he heads north to build a permanent Oblate mission. Arriving there Tuesday, May 12, 1863, he cheerily hires a few Indians to build a priest's house some 100 feet back from the sand beach. Yet when he and his fellow priest, Father Mourier, paddle back from their northern tour through the slime green dog-days, on August 8 they see only a pile of logs. Patiently they set to cut, fit and chink their house by October 12. And with laughter as they and Father Lebret endure the long winter: "All our furniture," Father Pian writes, "consists of one bench. We sleep on the floor our feet toward the chimney, with no fear of falling out of bed." Then in spring celebration of new life, Father Mourier baptizes Alfred Miron, the first baby born to a Canadian settler on Lake Temiskaming.

Fort Temiskaming

That older ways are passing is emphasized again when the new Hudson's Bay Company Governor, Alexander Dallas, decrees closing Lac des Allumettes post and opening a two man depot thirty miles upriver at des Joachims. A third clerk will stay in the village of Pembroke to buy any stray furs on the west side of the river, but stiff competition he expects from the two Murray brothers, fur merchants here for the past fifteen years.

As more settlers are moving upriver, steamboats, in 1864, follow to supply their community needs. And these boats offer a cheap alternative to the annual brigade of Montreal canoes. Bring down the Fort Temiskaming furs, Governor Dallas now orders, to the new des Joachims' steamship terminal and return with the Montreal supplies. But both Hector McKenzie and John Simpson, fearful of exposing innocent Temiskaming Indian paddlers to southern temptations and at the same time publicly advertising Temiskaming's wealth to more petty traders, defy Dallas. How much longer, though, can they make Temiskaming time stand still? The firm tone of George Dallas' letter last September already threatens time is short:

we are still carrying on our trade in the old fashion with fixed establishments, meant to be self-sustaining, as in the interior with farms cattle horses tradespeople &c attached. Such establishments in the Indian country are necessary and comparatively inexpensive: but as soon as settlement goes on around them, the cost of maintenance is increased and the posts themselves become really unnecessary; as our officers and servants can be more economically kept as boarders in hotels, - in fact the servants can be entirely dispensed with and the number of officers reduced. This is the proper way, I consider, to look at and deal with our Stations in the settled portion of Canada, which are no longer required as links in the line of communication. The simple question to decide is, when the proper time has arrived for abandoning the various posts.

7

Dragging Behind A Sack

That fur times are changing, Father Lebret, having just built a frame chapel at Mattawa, smilingly accepts. But so angry next summer is Hector McKenzie with the loss of his Lac des Allumettes-Fort William home he retires from the Hudson's Bay Company. He cannot deny, though, the permanent loss of his home and Company business to competition from surrounding settlers. Why even this same 1864 summer, while measuring the Township of Mattawa, the surveyor notes,

There are already at the Fort a large Catholic chapel, two good hotels, a Hudson's Bay Company general store, and on the Antoine, a couple of miles distant, Mr. McConnell's sawmill....There is as yet no grist mill, the high prices for hay and oats leading the few settlers there are to cultivate hardly anything else.

John Bangs with his uncle James' help is framing his own one and a half storey general store. And from now on, as Mattawa's first postmaster he will also sort the weekly mail relayed on from Joachim. Noah Timmins has built one of the hotels, the Western, for Mr. Durell. James Bangs is building the other for himself.

In July, Bishop Guiges, accompanied by Fathers Tortel and Gillies from Pembroke, lands at Mattawa where he says Mass and confirms twenty new members of the year-old church. Two days later they leave for Lake Temiskaming. On August 4 in full Sunday shine, Bishop Guiges consecrates Father Pian's Narrows beach site for the church of St. Claude Mission. And this evening, until the light finally fades at 10:00 o'clock, the faithful pile up stones for the foundation rectangle. By the end of the following week, a floor of pit-sawn planks level the sill beams, and log walls begin to rise. Antoine Thivierge from Mattawa and the Indian d'Ecrévisse donate their help. But saddened are they along with everyone else on both sides of the Narrows when they hear La Cave eddies have swallowed Rinaldo McConnell's canoe and, expert though he was, drowned his generous spirit.

By March 25, 1865, bare timbers glow yellow against the lake's blue-shadowed snow—St. Claude Mission chapel stands complete. Yet John Simpson leaves Fort Temiskaming and barely glances at it as a toboggan pulls him down to a doctor at Pembroke. Then despite his forty-seven year old body, skeleton-thin from chronic disease over the last few years, he returns as far as Fort William where on April 8 he falls off the wharf and drowns. Transferred from Eastmain, Robert Hamilton becomes head of Temiskaming district.

Immediately after moving into the old Fort, Hamilton sends two men up the lake to build a rival trade house beside Piché's store. Similar to Charles Stuart's tactic six years ago against the Bangses, Hamilton's Fort Wrath quickly puts Piché out of business. Despite the pleasure of Mrs Piché's knitted red toques and kitchen brewed beer the Indians believe false Hudson's Bay Company stories that Piché has smallpox. Even if he has, they still do not understand others have mostly died elsewhere from the disease when, hoping to end its fiery fever they stood for hours in bone chilling lakewater.

Unrepentant, Piché leapfrogs his family to the rocky point a mile north up Temiskaming shore and continues farming. And with the help of Thomas Murray's merchandise money from Pembroke, he resumes fur trading.

Fort Wrath does pursue him north, but Hamilton also has to worry about more petty traders interfering with the Abitibi Indians. In charge of Fort Abitibi, John Garton feels powerless against their magnetic prices. Especially embarrassed since his brother-in-law, Alex Dukis from Lake Nipissing, with the supply backing of Penetanguishene's fur merchant Alfred Thompson, has worked his way up through Lake Temagami and the Montreal River northwest into the Kenogamissi area. To challenge Dukis in September, Hamilton sends two men this time over the Matabanick portage up the Montreal River to its headwater Matchewan Lake. By October, Walter Faries comes down from Matawagamingue with two of his own men to take command of this new strategic outpost.

On their way back to Fort Temiskaming Hamilton's two men stop over at Matabanick, now a summer depot for lumberman Humphrey's horses. His shanty foremen, John and Bill Burns, are gathering the last stooks of hay from the six acre bush clearing some 100 yards up from the tree-fringed lakeshore. Beside the lean-to shack above the slope, green tops of carrots, potatoes and turnips still stick out of the ground. Fresh spring water weaves its narrow way along the bottom of a gully rumpling the north edge of the clearing. A rutted wagon road bumps down alongside it, down from the shack —curving back down to the scrub bush, clay mud, boulders and one tall pine by the beach.

Lumber Depot (Picturesque Canada)

During next year, 1866, Robert Hamilton finally ends the perennial fear of squatters settling the Company hayfields at the Head of the Lake, even the property of Fort Temiskaming itself. By October he will mail a surveyor's plan of the haymeadows and Narrows point along with a signed application of purchase to the Crown Lands office in Ottawa.

While living at the old Fort the surveyor praises the summer labourers squaring timber support posts — new bones for the old store. What he cannot understand, though, are the threadbare furnishings within the dwelling houses. Signs of a landlord's failing interest? Even Charles Stuart ridicules the lack of carpets, comfortable chairs, hardwood tables and the drab yellow walls. But so long as the buildings do not fall down, Robert Hamilton is content with Fort Temiskaming as a warehouse office rather than a permanent home.

Across the Narrows, though, the Grey nuns, Sisters Raisenne and Vincent, joyfully clean their new mission home. Now that the parsonage has a second floor they have private quarters downstairs. And when the priests move into next year's new parsonage, they will have this entire building to themselves — to serve as refuge, childrens' shelter, hospital and school.

All this within a new country under one Dominion. For in 1867 the Parliament in London, England, passes the British North America Act joining the Province of Canada with New Brunswick and Nova Scotia in Confederation. Since Quebec and Ontario once again split into separate provinces, the Hudson's Bay Company more than ever wonders how far north will extend different provincial land claims. Increasingly besieged by petty traders, the Company builds New Post on the Abitibi River, halfway between Fort Abitibi and Moose. Is this a planned retreat? How much longer before the old posts south of the Height of Land are left general stores at the mercy of encroaching settlements?

Very soon, Charles Stuart suggests, after he leaves Grand Lac in 1868 to replace Robert Hamilton who has transferred to Cumberland House. For in response to local settlers, Stuart, with a contract for $160.00 per year, opens a general post office at Fort Temiskaming. William Polson's son John does deliver the company's Montreal mail packets now, but only on the first of January and mid May on route to Moose Fort and its inland posts. Too outdated is this, though, for new settlers. With Stuart having mail brought up from Mattawa on the fourth or fifth day of every month, they can stay in touch with an outside world, which generally declares itself opposed to the Hudson's Bay Company's domination of their Temiskaming lives.

Mass In A Lumber Shanty   (*Picturesque Canada*)

In March, Father Nédelec adds his name to the missionaries' mailing address. And strong enough to preach his love for Temiskaming, Father

Laverlochère returns. On June 27, Sister St. Antoine arrives at the Narrows to take charge of the nuns' residence. She shudders at the black marks burnt into the back wall by flames from a May 31 forest fire. At least she or the eleven other sisters arriving in the summer will not have to remember the terror. Bachelor, Octave Saucier, clearing farmland on a lonely point seven miles down the eastern lakeshore and especially thankful to have their friendly hospital care close by, cheers their good fortune.

By 1869 Fort Temiskaming seems to have solved its problem of transporting supplies. Robert Hamilton, uncertain whether he could hire enough Indian paddlers for a des Joachim pickup, had argued for the lumbermans' winter haulage way to Lake Temiskaming. And if the Hudson's Bay Company wants to save money, he persisted, rather than sled the supplies all the twisting river way from Montreal, why not use the Brockville and Ottawa Railway to Sand Point? The Company agreed. So rather than use a Montreal contractor, the Company now hires Noah Timmins to haul the supplies up the winter route, east along Snake Creek to Obasking Lake then bend back to Joseph Miron's Opemika Narrows farm.

Better to have Noah Timmins working for us, the Company reasons: for over ten competitive years he has done too profitable a sideline business in furs at Mattawa. As a skilled lumberman he also contracted to build Durell's Western Hotel. But his first love is trading. And as furs have grown scarcer around Mattawa, he has often thought of moving north. And with the expensive value of food and fodder supplies to lumber shanties, why not open a combined general supplies and trade store on Lake Temiskaming? He could haul his supplies in and the furs out. Both Bangses' and Piché's attempts failed because they had no such general store method of making extra money to outbid the Hudson's Bay Company for furs. Similarly, Moïse Lavallée's penny-poor approach would have failed had he tried to operate on Lake Temiskaming. So just as the Hudson's Bay Company offered the Polsons and McBride a better deal than the Bangses', it talks Noah Timmins out of his clever trading scheme with more mail delivery money than he could ever hope to earn after the heavy expense of any Lake Temiskaming store.

But Timmins does not sit idle between deliveries. With his family now living at Mattawa Point, he promises Fathers Nédelec and Guéguen lodgings for the coming winter so they might keep their church and a school open. Not yet, the priests reply as their companion James Kelly also reminds them he has hired on to labour at their central mission house on Lake Temiskaming. From there they still have to reach out in equal directions to the wide parish of all Temiskaming. Soon, though, Mattawa will have a resident priest.

After twelve years absence Angus McBride brings his family down from New Post for a more central life among his Polson relatives at the Head of the Lake. Supplied with goods from Fort Temiskaming he will trade for furs from his Post des Quinze house at Point of Departure. Yet with word spreading of the Hudson's Bay Company sale of Rupert's Land to the Federal government, he knows his trading days may be numbered as more settlers will inevitably disrupt Temiskaming's wild natural ways. In the meantime, however, today's earliest settlers around Lake Temiskaming jockey for best farm locations as back and forth they go.

Joseph Miron, in 1870, shifts four miles north up the lake from Opemika to farm the point of eastside land Thomas Lalonde first cleared. Twenty-three miles farther up, Moïse Lavallée, who has quit his La Cave store, now farms the northeast section of the same bay De Troyes visited overnight on May 21, almost two-hundred years ago. Left behind by Lavallée's family at the foot of the Long Sault rapids is John England, settled with his family alongside Hyacinthe Charron.

Under the clouds of October 10 afternoon, though, further steps stop, when Hudson's Bay Company trader, James Hackland, recently transferred from Temagami post, drowns. A hundred yards off the old Fort's sand beach a sudden gust of northwest wind flips his canoe. Wife Ellen and her children shriek out the gate down to the wooden dock. Too late. All that remains is for him to be buried in the little Protestant cemetery William Garson has worked so hard to maintain behind the clerk's house—buried beside his son James who died eight years before.

Settlement pressure at the south end of Lake Temiskaming continues to build next summer. So busy is Mattawa, Fathers Nédelec and Poitras cannot reject Noah Timmins' latest offer of an old shed to use as a school for thirty pupils. To accommodate travellers into Lake Kipewa, Jacob Racicot nails together an Ottawa River hotel at Snake Creek. Charles Beavais, Georges Martineau and Bob Green stop over here on route to their homes on Kipewa's Beavais Bay. To keep a suspicious eye on any strangers detouring their fur trade way into Lake Temiskaming, however, Charles Stuart at the old Fort hires the American Civil War soldier Steve Lafricain to operate a trade store close to Joseph Miron. And more particularly to discourage Noah Timmins, who may still have trade-store ideas of his own.

In 1872, Octave Saucier sells his farm clearing halfway along the broad point just north of Lavallée's bay, to James Quinn, and packs himself south towards Opemica to settle on Point Antoine three miles below Lafricain's store. Like everyone else this summer he cannot solve the mysterious disappearance of four men paddling their canoe north over the deep waters of Lake Temiskaming. Towards the late evening of September 9, though, visitor Father Florent Vanderbergue and eighteen year old Brother Mofette safely land their canoe at the upper Narrows Mission. A few wigwams still linger along the cooling shore; their supper fires smoke orange sparks above. Brother Mofette sees oil lamp-kindled window panes in the black building shapes across the lake. And he remembers his promise to the Oblates in Ottawa to help light more wicks like these in Temiskaming.

But for now, the few settlers already here still find land to farm a difficult choice. Michael Thompson seems the exception, though, as he hums and hoes potatoes at the bottom of the first deep bay north of the old Fort.

Reversing Octave Saucier's most recent move south, Joseph Miron, in 1873, sells his farm to John McMartin and rafts his family up to live beside Moïse Lavallée. And after quitting the Hudson's Bay Company, Steve Lafricain soon follows to farm the northeast river mouth land left vacant by Onésime Salois Caya, in the broad bay next north of Lavallée's. Left behind near his empty store is the young widow of Eusèbe Quellet who drowned July 4.

Settler's Shanty (Picturesque Canada)

This same summer, since the earlier purchase of Rupert's Land has started a federal-provincial dispute over the exact lands belonging to Ontario, the Federal government begins an accurate survey of the Quebec-Ontario border north from the Head of Lake Temiskaming up to a presently adjudicated boundary set along the fifty-first parallel of latitude. Yet still maintaining that the land between this latitude line and James Bay never was part of Rupert's Land, Ontario protests further.

Even its predecessor, the Province of Canada, never accepted the Hudson's Bay Company's blanket claim to all the lands drained by the rivers into Hudson Bay. Why? Well think of ancient French claims to the northern Abitibi lands? And what other land claims did the early Montreal traders establish after fifty years of operating posts on Frederick House, Matawagamingue and Kenogamissi lakes? Remember both England and France had accepted Francis 1's three hundred year old principle that occupation and settlement established land rights in colonial America. The Hudson's Bay Company had been too late establishing its right to the land south of James Bay, Ontario argues.

Nevertheless, finding his own Canadian bush life way a young Englishman, Charles Cobbold Farr, has hired on at Pembroke as a $1.00 a day axeman with government surveyors, O'Dwyer and O'Hanley. And as the party in November canoes up the Ottawa River he meets numerous settlers. John McDougall's family at the foot of Flat Rapids dries and feeds their shivering bodies. A mile and a half above the Long Sault they stop at Baldwin's shanty. Fond memories of Rinaldo McConnell's days still warm a later conversation at Opemica Narrows. Passing Quellet's they see the young widow gathering wood along the shore. John McMartin entertains them. Edward Wright, whose father William owns the timber limits around Michael Thompson's farm and some twenty years ago rediscovered De Troyes' old lead-silver mine, is at the Opemica post office. While tracing the timber slide over the rocky eastern shoreline into the lake up from Bryson's Island, he tells them, the caulks on his father's boots scuffed off some galena. The whole rock surface seems to be a broad belt of green pudding stone glistening with blue metal fragments throughout. Unfortunately, ten tons of ore samples his father recently took out of the twelve foot deep exploration shaft slid off the raft into the Deux Rivières rapids.

Paddling next morning past the hundreds-of-feet high, east shore escarpment, Farr learns of the Picojeesies, the three inch to three foot fairies hiding among the broken rocks. Later in the day they touch the grassy landing just north of Kipewa River's rock jawed mouth. On this ground first cleared by J. Grenier, Bill Burns now lives . He has left Humphrey's Depot to count the logs chuting down from the lake above to form cribs bound for the United States and England. Next day the party crosses the lake to visit Jolicoeur's meadowed, Montreal River island home with Bonin's mainland farm behind. Farther on the small rocky island of Roche McLean clings to the west shore. Here over fifty years ago, the story goes, someone killed a North West Company man named McLean and threw his body into the lake. Back across the lake again and up the eastern shore is the Bay of Moose Wabik where Steve Lafricain now keeps company with a thirty foot diameter, moose shaped rock perched on a shoal. Then under the 400-foot-high cliff and past Little River, the party spurts around the point to Fort Temiskaming's warm shelter from this "bitterly cold day".

For three weeks they bed and cook in the Men's Houses, "little white-washed log-built boxes". Seeing Farr pull a sleigh along the bayshore collecting deadwood for the stoves, one of the old Fort clerks, A.G. Ryder, promises to tell Chief Trader Charles Stuart of Farr's desire for a better job.

Stuart "in his rough but not unkind manner" immediately offers Farr a Hudson's Bay Company chance, whenever he returns next spring from surveying the northern bush. And just in case he himself may not be here because of his planned retirement from the Company, Stuart will make sure his replacement, Colin Rankin, knows of the job offer. Much warmer now, Farr gathers more firewood while the lake turns to ice.

Fort Temiskaming

St. Claude Mission - Lake Temiskaming Narrows -

Too thin the ice is in the Narrows, though. On December 12, Antoine Thivierge chances a short walk from the Oblates' mission to the Hudson's Bay Company store and post office. Halfway over where the rough current rasps, Thivierge breaks through and under the jagged edge.

A trembling week later the surveyors dare their own footsteps. Leaving the boats under cover of old Fort sheds they avoid the Narrows' shell ice and, with Brother Mofette guiding a safer way north, tramp forward tugging toboggan loads of transits, tools, tents, bedding and food. Then snow begins to fall and a crack booms open down the middle of the jumping lake. Past the few gray buildings shuddering out on Wabi's wind swept point they veer right, up to Angus McBride's Point of Departure house. Soon, a hut stove sizzles their Christmas meal of salt pork beside a steaming pot of plum pudding. This night while McBride's lame horse shivers in its lone stable, their healthier legs kick to joyous jigs fiddled in the low, lamplighted room of McBride's shaking house.

In the morning O'Hanley summarizes, for page thirty-four of next year's government report, his glimpse of settlement on this upper lake,

a settler in Heenan Bay [one mile south of Montreal Island], a lumber depot and farm on the Montreal owned by Messrs Bell and Hickey; a settler, Mr.J.B. Jolioeux [sic] on Montreal Island, and two or three Norwegian settlers on the Mattapisewan [Matabitchuan]. In Ontario at the Narrows opposite Fort Temiskaming a Roman Catholic Mission presided over by four other clergymen and two Friars. Opposite is Fort Temiskaming, one of the Hudsons Bay Company's principal forts in charge of a chief trader. An Indian settler, Wabikiyak on the point called after him.

Then on to their northern chore the party goes, forty-two miles of bush lines to cut and survey, with a cut-stone marker left every mile along the Quebec-Ontario boundary from the Head of Lake Temiskaming to the Height of Land.

Next May, Colin Rankin does assure C.C. Farr of a Hudson's Bay Company place by summer's end. Across the Narrows, the priests and nuns still talk of Bishop Guiges' February 8 death and his possible replacement. Back at Pembroke with a season's pay in pocket C.C. Farr forgets the harsh winter and enjoys a rest, closer to the quiet Suffolk ways of his Church of England minister father. And he romances young Louisa Georgina Probyn. In August, as he must return to Fort Temiskaming he chooses instead of the stagecoach, to take the Union Forwarding Company's new steamer service from des Joachims to Mattawa. Captain Mulligan of the *Mattawan* reminds him he can later pay Louis, the Indian mail courier, $2.50 for a canoe ride on his weekly trip from Mattawa to the old Fort. On October 3, Farr writes a letter to his sister Fanny in England explaining his Company duties, from "nine in the morning to six in the evening my business is to trade with the Indians, to see that the men employed do their work, and to look after things in general.'' Soon a Hudson's Bay Company postmaster, he leaves to manage Hunter's Lodge, bidding for furs against the petty traders, shantymen and settlers of Lake Kipewa. This time he paddles with Louis and the mail without paying a cent.

Des Joachims Landing (Picturesque Canada)

Although deep in the winter bush, Farr learns the Federal and Ontario governments will set up a three man commission to settle the boundary dispute. In the meantime they will accept the fifty-first parallel of latitude as the northern boundary with the Dominion owning the land beyond. Of little present importance is this to Farr, though, when he smells forest fires next spring.

Cinders from burning stumps west of St. Claude Mission cause separate blazes May 23 and 28. But luckily the ground is still moist enough to slow any leaping spread. Brother Mofette knows they must be more careful, however, especially as the Oblate order is buying 1,000 more neighbouring acres. Across the lake and north at Michael Thompson's farm clearing, where James Kelly lives in his root cellar hermitage with its bark roof over cedar logs, another fire starts. The southwest wind blows it away from the old Fort but by the time it runs out of fuel at the Quinze River, few trees remain up the eastern shore of Lake Temiskaming. Yet the clay soil has suffered little and Brother Mofette consoles Kelly. And he humours him later with the October 25 story of a harmless chimney fire in the Mission parsonage. Three days later Bishop Duhamel takes over the diocese. And when Octave Saucier marries young widow Quellet, all seems right with the world.

So much so, in 1876, the Oblates start to build a larger church on the flattened garden space above the priests' house, away from the damp ground of the beach. And so eagerly during winter do they hammer together the fifty by twenty-five foot frame structure, by March 12 the newest church of Saint Claude steeple peaks sharply against the evergreen background hill, a beacon for Bishop Duhamel when he first arrives on August 14. Also for the Indians who arrive the day after from all directions for their most sacred day of the year. Once the Bishop has celebrated Mass the whole congregation flocks up the flag canopied path to kneel at the top of the hill and look out from under maple and wild cherry trees onto the round blue lake below. And Joseph Miron prays he will not have to move his family ever again from their latest home two miles south down the Quebec shore, beside the Little River. An unnecessary prayer, though? If what Camille Latour says is any indication, Miron may be running out of places to move. In charge of his brother Oliver's sawmill at Mattawa for the last three years Latour has just paid $160.00 for 320 inland acres west of the Oblate Mission's additional square mile acreage at Pointe à la Barbe. Already Camille has started to clear land along a south-flowing creek and plans a 22 by 26 foot log house, 30 by 40 foot frame barn and 20 by 30 foot frame barn and 20 by 30 foot frame storehouse.

And he talks of how Mattawa is mushrooming. Noah Timmins with partner Gorman from Pembroke has finally opened his general store there. And John Loughrin from Renfrew, who previously clerked for Messrs. T. and W. Murray, the same fur merchants who bankrolled Piché's store battle against Fort Wrath, now works for them. More and more people are moving north up the Ottawa. How many of them will just keep coming up to Lake Temiskaming?

At the Head of the Lake on Wednesday, February 27, 1878, William Polson dies. Eighty-six years old, his faithful memory reached back to the North West Company and Hudson's Bay Company feud. Colin Rankin sets the Union Jack at halfmast and arranges for his spring burial in the Roman Catholic cemetery, atop the ridge behind Fort Temiskaming.

With Big Louis, the mailman, C.C. Farr runs the rapids down to Mattawa, then steps aboard Olivier Latour's steamboat for Pembroke where he enters Holy Trinity Anglican church, on July 23, to marry eighteen year old Georgina Probyn. Back up river with Basil Antoine steering their honeymoon canoe, they reach Hunter's Lodge with no food but wedding cake crumbs.

More relaxed with married life Farr is still reminded, on August 3, of his winter exertions four years ago: Alexander MacKenzie's federal government has finally decided the northern Ontario border starting in the west will include the English and Albany rivers, follow the coast of James Bay east to the meridian of Lake Temiskaming and south along the present Ottawa River mid-channel line. Yet after the October 17 election when Sir

John A. MacDonald's Conservatives win power, Parliament will refuse to pass this boundary legislation. Only James Kelly seems able to make any kind of definite decision anywhere, as he abandons his underground hermitage on Lake Temiskaming's boundary line for a stand-up life of boating work on Kipewa Lake.

Next February 4, Brother Lapointe, tramping back to the Mission Narrows from his search for firewood, stumbles over a frozen son of the Wabenicikabe family. Out hunting rabbits he must have lost direction in a snowstorm, fallen with his snowshoes still tied on and rolled face up with mittened hands across his chest. John Piché spends the 1879 summer building a grist mill at the first tumble of water on the fast running creek one mile south of Humphrey's Depot. Looking across the lake to the Quebec shore he sees white smoke clouding upwards from his father's stump fires. Their battle against Fort Wrath is a dim memory. And fifty-year-old stories of huge brigades trooping furs up the lake to Moose Factory seem incredible today. A few canoes pass but most impressive now is the odd timber raft in full sail heading south.

Yes, even these rafts are fewer. Baptiste Jolicoeur's June burial in the old Fort's Roman Catholic cemetery stirs further stories of Lake Temiskaming's taller timber days. Colin Rankin, Chief Factor since the first of this month, then reminds his two clerks, John Cummings and George Simpson, of the feuding McConnells. George, though, has a more haunting memory of his sister Marie Louise's burial years ago in this same ground. Warehouseman David McLaren sees the Bonin's rowboat carrying Jolicoeur's coffin cross the Narrows from the Mission church, yet he must stay in the store sorting the weekly mail. William Petrault lugging iron bars over to John Turner's blacksmith shop watches the priests lead pallbearers up over the worn bank past the old chapel to the graveyard above. John Morrison would have wanted to pay his last respects but he left last week to take over Hunter's Lodge while C.C. Farr and McConnor moved to Bryson's Depot.

A week later a stranger paddles by. Having created in 1872 the judicial district of Nipissing, Ontario now takes advantage of a recent boundary award to push its northern limits on to James Bay. And has therefore appointed Edward Borron a stipendiary magistrate to smooth the push. After fourteen years in the mines of Scotland, Borron came to Canada in 1850 and since then has worked five years as general manager of Bruce Mines, a prospector, mining inspector and four years Member of Parliament for Algoma District. So he understands this northern land of Indians and fur traders; he knows the law must not impose order too quickly on their free spirited lives nor show disrespect for the Hudson's Bay Company's historic sense of feudal pride. By also appointing Nipissing District's Hudson's Bay Company officers as justices of the peace, Ontario hopes they might begin to exchange loyalties with the province.

Although they have left the front door facing Lake Temiskaming open, Brothers Mofette and Ferdinard Verrette are too busy straightening pews inside the Oblate's newest mission church to notice Magistrate Borron's passage north. While sunlight streams through the three south side windows, making their arched frames even lighter blue, and spills over the imitation cut stone walls, the Brothers talk of sledding by February ice from Mattawa a statue of the Virgin Mary and a bell for the steeple. No miracle this, since John Piché brought his mill stones the same way last winter.

After March 2, 1880, the angelus tolls its daily reminder over Temiskaming Narrows. Even Brother Mofette claims in June while digging his church garden at Kelly's Bay he can hear the bell. Too far away though is Adam Burwash while clearing farmland at the Head of the Lake. So, too, the following winter are Remi Martel and his brother-in-law, Remi Filteau, cutting logs there for Olivier Latour. No time do they have to listen anyway. Hustling after $1.25 a day for one man with two horses or 60 cents for one man alone, they must get ready to float the logs next spring through the Mission Narrows down the Long Sault to Mattawa.

In late June, 1881 Charles Paradis, for the last ten years an art teacher at the Oblate's Ottawa College, arrives at Saint Claude Mission. But he does not come just to listen to the bell. Barely over five feet tall yet a husky thirty-three years old, he wants to travel as much of this Temiskaming country as summer holidays will allow.

Father Paradis' Drawing Of Lake Temiskaming Mission Narrows

On his canoe way to visit Indians at the Head of the Lake, Father Paradis glimpses the clearing and small retreat house Brother Mofette is building for the priests at Kelly's Bay. Then on July 19 comes an exciting opportunity, as trapper Rastoul with four Indian companions beaches his canoe at the Mission and asks for priests to visit Temagami and Matachewan. Surely, he says, after a fifteen year's absence you owe the few Roman Catholic converts surviving there a service. Accompanying Father Mourier, Father Paradis follows Rastoul back up the Matabitchuan to Rabbit Lake, to Whitebear Lake, over a short portage into Lake Temagami and southwest down its narrow arm to Bear Island. There, on Saturday, August 13, in front of John Turner's Hudson's Bay Company post, Father Mourier plants a wooden cross. Then up to Anima Nipissing Lake for the long portage down hill to the Bay Lake section of the Montreal River they go on their remaining trip to Matachewan.

John Turner And Wife

Meanwhile, Bishop Duhamel is again visiting the Temiskaming mission field. Having left Ottawa on July 25 with Abbé J.B. Proulx and Father Robert, the bishop rode the Canadian Pacific Railway to its latest end at Klock's Mills. From there Captain Mulligan steamboated them upriver. After Fathers Déléage and Emery had taken them to meet the settlers along Mattawa River west to Lake Talon, eight Algonquins in a specially painted thirty foot canoe paddled them up to Lake Temiskaming. They paddled a load of seven passengers as Fathers Laverlochère and Mourier (a week before he left on his Temagami trip), scholastic Brothers Blais and Cahill and lay

Brother Débigarre had come down from Temiskaming to welcome and accompany the bishop north. By August 2, seven o'clock in the evening, fifty Indian canoes buzzed the queen bee canoe from Pointe à la Barbe to Saint Claude Mission.

Here under the supervision of Father Pian, daily life has settled into a devout pattern. Fathers Laverlochère and Mourier serve the immediate Lake Temiskaming region. Father Nédelec visits the missions of Abitibi, Hudson Bay, Fort William and Golden Lake. Father Guéguen visits Grand Lac, Lac Barrière, the Gatineau and St. Maurice. For the sake of their health the two scholastic brothers, Blais and Cahill, have lived here for the past two years. Amongst other duties Brother Cahill is in charge of the boys' school. The three lay brothers, Mofette, Verrette and Débigarre, maintain the Old Mission buildings and work the two mission farms. While Sister St. Antoine supervises sisters St. Vincent and Christine de Jésus tending hospital patients, Sister Colombe de Jésus teaches the girls' school.

From this central mission house in two smaller canoes the bishop's party, now joined by Chief Factor Rankin from the Old Fort across the Narrows, continues on to Father Nédelec's 371 Abitibi Mission Indians. With Okacin as pilot and William Cromalty as steersman, Salomon Massinikijik, brothers Joachim and Jean Wabikijik, eighteen year old orphan Pierrot Thivierge paddle the bishop's canoe. Pilot Pierre Pénassi, steersman William Petras, paddlers M. Harry, Colin Rankin's son on summer holidays from his Toronto school, W. Clauston, J. Stinger, M. Thompson and John Polson propel Colin Rankin's. When the bishop asks to see Wright's Mine, Colin Rankin orders the canoes away from the middle of the lake to hug the eastern shore. This "is the first time, to my knowledge," Father Pian remarks, "that Mr. Rankin deviated from a straight line." On their later way to Angus McBride's Point of Departure farm, they wave at lay brothers Mofette and Verrette cutting wild hay in the Chenal du Diable mouth of the Blanche River. More and more, Bishop Duhamel is convinced the Oblates should start settling these fertile lake lands, in the same organized way they have been doing for the last twenty years in the Eastern Townships of Quebec.

Abbé Proulx, in one of eight letters to his fellow priest J.O. Routhier of Ste Anne, describes their first view of the Abitibi Mission; brilliant in August sunshine the chapel's tin sheeted steeple peaks like silver prayer hands into an everlasting blue. Together out on a low peninsula are Trader Henderson's Hudson's Bay Company house and the Roman Catholic church:

With [Henderson's] front porch half hidden behind a great hedge of aspens; in front of the main door is a garden of onions, turnips, cabbage and red currant bushes covered in berries; to the side are six other buildings which serve as store, storage sheds and dwellings for the company employees. Three acres away is the chapel on a height of ground overlooking the fort;...it is forty-two by twenty feet and behind is attached a little vestry room where the missionary lives. Above the fort, as a sign of rejoicing, flies the English flag...red; in front of the chapel flies the French blue.

The happiest Hudson's Bay Company man to meet Bishop Duhamel is old Aubichon, a Canadian from Sorel who has been here for the last forty-five years. Nowadays he does light chores for Mr. Miller, the Company warehouseman.

Fort Abitibi Looking West

Fort Abitibi Looking East

Fort Abitibi Dock

Camped between the fort and the church, Abitibi Indians crowd the pathway holding their babies out for the bishop's blessing. Their tent homes are "not large, eight by eight, the household goods are few, a trunk, a few covered, a stove, a cooking pot; nothing more than when it is necessary to move the owner in a quarter of an hour can pack his baggage and stow it all in the bottom of his canoe."

By the August 16 time the bishop returns to Lake Temiskaming, he has confirmed ninety-eight people. On their canoe way back down the lake, out past Wabi's Point, Abbé Proulx thrills, "the lake is overcast, as far as the eye can see the massive waves at least six feet high their crests like white manes fly from an army of galloping horses." And William Cromalty in quiet command steers through the spray.

At the Old Mission ceremony, Hilarion Massinikijik, chief of the Temiskaming Indians, makes Bishop Duhamel a band member. After the singing and dancing stops, Father Guéguen translates the bishop's thanks and offer of a banquet feast. Chief Massinikijik smilingly accepts, "Each native home is in joy, the heart, the spirit and the stomach."

Equally joyful Father Paradis will be after his October ordination in Ottawa when he gives thanks for next year's assignment to Lake Temiskaming. More so when Bishop Duhamel tells him the Quebec government has promised to lay out a township there for orderly settlement. But suddenly uncertain of their 1882 futures are the clerks at Old Fort Temiskaming. With the Canadian Pacific tracks now reaching Mattawa, the

Hudson's Bay Company has decided to shift its Temiskaming headquarters next year to this railhead supply base. So for the first time in its fur trading history the Old Fort will shrivel to outpost stature. With not too much loss of pride, though, C.C. Farr hopes as after nine years on Lake Kipewa he prepares to take command of the Old Fort as soon as Colin Rankin makes Mattawa his headquarters home.

This 1882 year of change starts with the unexpected January 24 death of Hilarion Massinikijik at the broad scoop of bay immediately north of Kelly's. One of his last looks was of Monz-o-mintick (Moose), the large island opposite shimmering in hoar frost. His Temiskaming ancestors had used it and the other upper lake islands as common property to pitch their tents and hunt when assembling for their annual spring reunions. Chief Island further north was the ancient ground where the band chief most often of the Massinikijik family had a regular camp. The other six families of Head of the Lake peoples would holiday on the remaining islands where space and game were equally plentiful. Today these island reserves may be forgotten but not the night's sky and its sparkling Milky Way where Indians believe Hilarion Massinikijik now journeys along his final "spirit path".

Temiskaming Indian Families

Families and Hunting Territories of the Timiskaming Indians.

No.	Family Name.	Translation.	Totem.	Hunting District.	Remarks.
1	Mazi'ni·gi·'jik	"Striped coloured sky"	Kingfisher.	West of Lake Timiskaming between Matabitchuan river, Rabbit lake, and Ottertail river.	The leading family of this band usually furnishes the chief.
2	Wa'bi·gi·'jik.	"White sky."	Caribou.	Northwest of Lake Timiskaming, basin of Wabi creek.	
3	Wɑdawe·'sis.	"Game animals hunt."(?)	Kingfisher.	East of Dawson point north of Quinze river to outlet of Quinze lake.	Also known as Ma'kɑde·'nin·i "Black Man," on account of his dark colour.
4	Ogu'cen.	"Son" (derivation).	(?)	East of Lake Timiskaming, south of Quinze river to line of Ville Marie.	Family extinct in male line.
5	Ka'tci·dji.	Derivation of "small."	(?)	South of Ogu'cen almost to Kipawa river.	He had a brother of same name belonging to Matachewan band (family also extinct).
6	Wa·beni'oªa'bi	"White Indian."	Kingfisher.	South of Wa'bi·gi·'jik to Bay lake.	These two were brothers who had received share of father's territory.
7	Kitci·'bi·en.	(?) "Big Pierre," or possibly derived from baby talk.	Kingfisher.	West of Lake Timiskaming to Montreal river and Bay lake.	

Returning from an instructional trip to Ottawa, Father Nédelec precedes Father Paradis off the train at Mattawa. Within days should come the final breakup of ice, but there is no canoeman available to take them north. So for guidance, food and cover, they volunteer to help twenty men tug the sixty-six foot long hull of Olivier Latour's steamer *Mattawan* up the rapids to Lake Temiskaming. As the boat can no longer make money monopolizing the passenger and freight run from des Joachim north, it might as well try to recover success farther upriver, away from C.P.R. competition. Over the calmer river waters the Fathers help row and pole; through the rapids with windlass and cables they tow from shore. Six back breaking days it takes to drag the boat up the Long Sault's six miles. Then on May 24, the battered hull floats free on Lake Temiskaming. But as its cracked keel and broken rudder will take two weeks to fix and with no missionary time to spare, Fathers Nédelec and Paradis flee northwards in a little skiff.

After a few days rest at Mission Narrows both men climb into an Indian canoe bound for the Head of the Lake where they celebrate Sunday Mass with 100 shantymen. Father Nédelec is to return to his Abitibi church. Father Paradis is to investigate the extent of Temiskaming settlement land all the way to the Bay. But up the Quinze Lake trail, while one Indian guide gossips about glittering silver and gold showings in the surrounding hills, Father Paradis grows fever weak. Finally unable to stumble on, he returns to Lake Temiskaming.

And here Father Pian tells him of the *Mattawan's* steamwhistle hooting its first June 4 arrival as Captain Mulligan dropped anchor off the old Fort's south shore dock. Like a taunt it was, Father Pian chuckles. Obviously the steamboat can only hasten the arrival of permanent settlers but the Hudson's Bay Company pretended indifference. How, though, can it conceal its dismay when a week later Quebec government surveyor James Rooney rows ashore from the *Mattawan* to chain out a surrounding township to be named after Bishop Duhamel. A block of land stretching ten miles inland, it will front the lake from Joseph Miron's Little River mouth to Wright's Mine. And after this, Rooney is to measure another equally large canton of Guiges stretching to the Head of the Lake.

Although saw log lumbermen throng the lake they stay only as long as it takes to remove the trees. And many of them are being lured away by the untouched timber forests of western Ontario. Not the permanent settlers, however. Groping inland through the newly surveyed cantons, they will stay to trample the Old Fort's Temiskaming fur farm flat.

So be it then, Father Paradis chants; wish the Hudson's Bay Company goodbye. Born at Kamouraska, he has vowed to restore French Catholic faith in Quebec's future. We must keep expanding its farmland size, he preaches, especially into this Temiskaming country so like his Saguenay home. Think of what the Commissioner of Crown Lands of Canada wrote in his 1856 Report about this region:

...high hills prevail on both sides of the river to the distance of halfway up Lake Temiskaming, where, from being mountainous, the country falls in a sudden step to a lower level of undulating hills with wide valleys generally of a clayey soil.

This lower country is well adapted for settlement, it extends up to the head of the lake, and to a yet undetermined distance beyond it. The River Blanche and other tributaries falling into the head of the lake, flow far through rich alluvial valleys."

Sharing the Oblate vision, Father Pian blesses Father Paradis and Brother Mofette as they row a kicking horse across the lake to plough a model farm beside the priests' house on Kelly's Bay. And while they are at it, why not rename this site Baie des Pères? Certainly it seems destined because of their efforts to be the distribution headquarters of Quebec province's newest colony. And the twenty-seven mile tote road Alex Dupont is stumping clear for Allan Grant's shantymen to shortcut from here to Lac des Quinze, can only help make it easier for settlers trekking into Duhamel and Guiges.

This 1882 summer, Charles Smith of Mattawa also sets about reshaping the landscape east. At the north end of Lake Kipewa, he is stretching a wooden dam across the main outlet river to reduce its heavy flow down into Lake Temiskaming. So blocked, the lake's increased height of water can find a southern outlet down a smooth sluice to Pike Lake fifty feet below and a final drop, 250 feet down the mile length of Gordon Creek. No longer now will the bashing rapids of northern Kipewa River mutilate logs beyond commercial use. Skilled in salvaging saw log profits, Smith and his brother, Tom, ten years ago scoured E. Varin's and David Moore's cut-over timber limits along the Mattawa River. Moore had bought and shifted farther west on to Edward Wright's five mile limit at the end of Duncan Sinclair's survey trail beside Lake Nipissing.

In addition to this present dam-building job, Charles Smith with partner Isaac hires Joe Miron to cut beam and planking wood at the Head of Lake Temiskaming, enough to build the paddle wheel steamer, *Argo*. Alex Lumsden has promised to buy this ship for towing log booms after Smith proves it can float next spring. Not only will it be a tugboat but also a second steamship for carrying settlers to our northern colony, Father Paradis enthuses. And when he hears that on September 22 Bishop Fabre has endorsed the creation of the new apostolic vicarate of Pontiac, with Bishop N. Zéphirin Lorrain's pledge to speed up settlement there and in this more northern mission of Temiskaming, he rejoices. Then he remembers Quebec colonizer Father Labelle's pleas, one evening last December in the Hotel Beaulieu at St. Jérôme: a public plea to continue the Montreal-St.Jérôme railway past Mont Laurier straight through to Lake Temiskaming. Too many surplus sons of Quebec, Father Labelle reminded his audience, are being squeezed out of their narrow family farms along the St. Lawrence, south across the American border into the empty and available lands of New

England. We must continue making room for them in their own home province, he pleaded.

October 1, Saint Claude Mission loses Father Pian to Ottawa. Too tired to face another Narrows winter, he hands control over to Father Déléage who arrives from Mattawa on November 5 with news the Canadian Pacific tracks are pushing west towards Lake Nipissing.

Railways! Steamships! Prepare for a larger congregation on Lake Temiskaming! Certainly the harmonium bought from Pratt and Boucher in Montreal, sledded from the railway station at Mattawa and placed behind the altar screen in Saint Claude church will fetch all settlers' ears. Thank, though, Colin Rankin's young Protestant daughter Elsa, the Indians call Okimakijigok meaning queen of the day, who is the only local person able to play it.

In 1883, to cut wood for Olivier Latour, Joseph Jodouin moves with his family from Mattawa to Opemica Narrows. With Captain Mulligan transferred to another steamboat on Lake Kipewa, Captain Blondin sees Jodouin's belongings ashore. Then he wheels the *Mattawan* north so passenger Paul Dumais can finish the survey of Duhamel and Guiges cantons. East of Guiges at the end of the long bay dangling south from Lac des Quinze, John Morrison is building a trade store. Gillies Lumber Company is counting on Alex Dupont's access road nosing out close to this location. And though he is mainly after a dwindling trade in furs, Morrison's well stocked store will help supply shantymen's food, clothing and fodder needs.

Far south of here, since Charles Smith's upper dam has raised the water level of Lake Kipewa, the Gordon Creek Improvement Company organizes to build a wooden chute along the boulder strewn creek bed, to channel sawlogs in a free rush of water down to the bottom end of Lake Temiskaming. Then, though it takes at least six hours for anyone strong enough to struggle up around the Long Sault rapids, logs can shoot down to Seven League Lake in half an hour, and on to Lumsden's, Latour's, Gillies', Klock's sawmills at Mattawa and beyond.

Although busy with Brother Mofette and newly arrived Brother Nicolas Proulx tilling land at Baie des Pères, Father Paradis still finds time to guide Father Gendreau, the treasurer for Ottawa College, on a tour of Lake Temiskaming. Responsible for much of the colonizing success in Quebec's Eastern Townships, Father Gendreau arrives on July 27. And Temiskaming amazes him. So abundant was last year's Baie des Pères' harvest, Brother Mofette has built a storage barn there. This year's fields promise much more. Sun-filled weeks heat the black soil and thousands of more stone-free acres wait under a second growth of bush stretching north, south and east. Listening later to Father Gendreau's experienced praise, Bishop Duhamel feels sure he should now campaign all-out for colonization here.

That Mattawa becomes an official village this year advertises the solid strength of northern settlement. Some 160 families vote William Hogarth mayor with Dr. Earl, William Murphy, Henry Timmins, J.A. Fink, and George Smith councillors. With three to four thousand lumbermen disturbing the village peace, with the Hudson's Bay Company headquarters there, with three churches, a hospital, school, prison and 600-foot-long Ontario Government bridge across the Mattawa River, the village inspires Lake Temiskaming's colonization growth.

Talk of inspiration! What of the 373 Canadian loggers and shantymen commanded by General Wolseley who have just left Ottawa to paddle British troops up the Nile to rescue General Gordon's garrison from the Mahdi at Khartoum? Wolseley said these northerners were the only men with enough strength and skill to overcome the Nile's fierce currents.

Father Paradis' Drawing of Mattawa - 1882 -

More inspiration? What of the red stained rocks exposed in the Canadian Pacific's cut through a little hill at recently named Sudbury Junction? Overhearing railway blacksmith Tom Flanagan describe ·this possible copper discovery and seeing for himself red mud along the tracks, John Loughrin, who is now junior partner with old associates Thomas and William Murray in their general store at Mattawa, and who also has his own supply contract for ties with the railway, forms a February 25, 1884, syndicate with the Murray brothers and Henry Abbot of Brockville. They buy discovery lot eleven's 310 acres in concession five of McKim township, at $1.00 per acre. A waste of money? Not after May 18, it seems, when Tom Frood will prospect another mineral discovery at the township's north end.

Nor are members of the Federal Parliament shy about other north country prospects either. In March, 1884, debate, Mr. Dawson, member for Algoma District, opens discussion on the value of Northern Ontario:

The late Walter McOuat says in his Geological Report for 1872: 'The whole region extending northward from the mouth of the Montreal River, which is about thirty miles south of the head of Lake Temiskaming, may be pretty correctly described as a level clay plain, with a great number of rocky hills and ridges protruding through it'.

Wanting more than faint praise, though, Peter White, member for North Renfrew, adds:

I know, that as a matter of fact, that on the shores of Lake Temiscaming, both in the Province of Ontario and the Province of Quebec, wheat of the very best quality has been grown and there is at present a grist mill...used for the grinding of wheat grown by the settlers.

Yet even these words pale beside Father Paradis' personal description on March 22 when he presents Bishop Duhamel with his pamphlet, *La région du Temiskaming,* which reads in part:

The soil of Témiscamingue is of a richness unequalled in the entire Ottawa valley. A grey earth, black and yellow; not a single stone over some twenty to thirty square miles. Other considerable stretches are grass lands easy to drain or better still vast burned over areas where the trees are uprooted and thrown down. A remarkable thing: in very few places does the earth appear to have suffered from the heat of the fire, the humus is perfectly intact and six to eight inches deep everywhere.

Father Paradis details the Quebec side of the lake, but what about Ontario's?

Isolated by the Canadian Pacific Railway's bypass of their city on its rich way west, the businessmen of Toronto have begun looking at the undeveloped lands of their own province to make up for lost fortunes elsewhere. With the Northern Railway to Gravenhurst now being lengthened by the Ontario Pacific Junction Railway tracks to Callander on Lake Nipissing, Toronto lobbies the Ontario government to continue this extension north across the Canadian Pacific right-of-way straight up into Temiskaming. Open up this remote country for agricultural settlement and the seaport advantage of James Bay, the businessmen chorus.

And the Dominion Parliament does grant them a charter for the Nipissing and James Bay Railway. From Callander station it will run 350 miles north skirting the west shores of Lakes Temiskaming and Abitibi, down the Abitibi River valley to Moose Factory — "From Lake Nipissing to within thirty miles of James Bay there is land of excellent quality, this is particularly noticeable in the neighbourhood of Lake Temiskaming." And Magistrate Borron has spoken of the enormous peat beds averaging eight to twenty feet thick near James Bay. On April 29, *The Globe* newspaper of Toronto reports President of the Lake Nipissing and James Bay Railway Company, W.B. McMurrich's boast, "the country north of Calender [sic] around Lake Temiskaming is suitable for settlement and branch road to Lake Temiskaming will make the valuable timber lands in that vicinity tributary to Toronto." Not as passionate, maybe, as Father Paradis' words but nevertheless confident.

For now, though, neither Quebec nor Ontario has the colonization advantage. One has surveyed lands to sell and the other has promised a railway. Each province needs both. Think, though, of Quebec's head-start if Father Paradis' settlers could have the railroad means of reaching Lake Temiskaming's ready land. Wishful thinking? Unfortunately yes, for the merchants of Montreal, content with their rich Canadian Pacific connection west, still refuse to support Father Labelle's three-year-old pleas for a branch colonization line up the eastern shore of Lake Temiskaming.

But without such a road, how many Quebec settlers have the strength to battle Ottawa River rapids from Mattawa to Lake Temiskaming? Will they have to wait instead for Ontario's railway to carry them in a roundabout way to the townships of Duhamel and Guiges? Unthinkable! says Father Paradis.

Better to flood the rapids below Lake Temiskaming, he suggests. If we build a dam at les Érables and remove the more gigantic boulders plugging the Long Sault, a twenty-two foot deep rush of water from Lake Temiskaming will raise the Ottawa River's water level by thirty-two feet. Then with the Long Sault and Mountain Rapids gone, steamboats could puff their uninterrupted way north from les Érables to the Head of the Lake. A seven mile spur line from the C.P.R. station at Mattawa would be sufficient to bring settlers, luggage and supplies to the wharf at Lake Temiskaming's newly created south end port.

Lucky to have already reached the lake over cracked winter ice, Remi Martel settles beside a small creek just south of a sharp point of land across the lake from Bonin's Montreal River farm. Also across from the Anderson farm on the south side of the same Montreal River. Swarmed are these Ontario acres by the neighbouring Bell-Hickey land development where horses graze the broad ribbon of meadow rolling on south to the Matabitchuan. And farther down the shore from this river's mouth, standing on his own patch of hayland, bachelor Aaron Jonason welcomes the warm company of the Martel's night-time fire flickering from the far shore.

The Oblates twenty year record of dates winter ice completely left Lake Temiskaming:

1865	May	06	1870	Apr	25	1875	May	15	1880	May	15
1866	May	15	1871	May	08	1876	May	08	1881	May	09
1867	May	16	1872	May	15	1877	May	12	1882	May	13
1868	May	17	1873	May	12	1878	May	10	1883	May	08
1869	May	12	1874	May	26	1879	May	18	1884	May	07

Departing Mattawa June 12, Fathers Paradis and Proulx accompany Bishop Lorrain on his first visit up Lake Temiskaming. Colin Rankin salutes as their canot de maître, bearing the bishop's name of Zéphire on its bow, starts upriver for La Cave. Okacin in front sets pace for his six other Temiskaming paddlers. At Abitibi they pick up resident Father Nédelec and continue on for Moose Factory and Fort Albany missions. Along the Abitibi River, though, because of a bitter personal quarrel with Father Nédelec, Father Paradis threatens to turn back alone. But despite his rage, a single mindedness, overzealous perhaps, for seeing all of Temiskaming pushes him on.

Opemican

Meanwhile, settlement on Lake Temiskaming creeps forward. Captain Jones docks at Opemica Narrows to open a government post office, Opemican, in Joseph Jodouin's house. Five miles east of Baie des Pères, beside Dupont's Road, Thomas Larouche from Chicoutimi arrives June 4, quickly grubhoes six charred acres clean even of stumps, sows ten minots of grain and on July 6 watches his cornflowers ripen while he eats fresh potatoes. With a log house, small barn, two cows and hens, his family will be secure for the winter. Shanties to the east offer $30.00 a ton for his surplus hay—add this money to the winter wages he can earn working as lumberjack, and his family might soon enjoy a larger house.

Not so balanced living alone across the lake up the Ontario shore at Matabanick, though, is Louis Sirouin. Having worked here after Paddy Ryan took over Humphrey's original depot farm from Egan, Louis decided to remain after the rest of Ryan's crew vacated. A lonely squatter's life it is, weeding a small, hillside garden, but he can look forward to winter work with Ryan's men now cutting to the west on Montreal River. So tall and solitary is the tree at the lakeshore landing spot below his small farm, people passing on the lake refer to his homesite as the "Big Pine".

August 4 saddens Lake Temiskaming with Father Laverlochère's death. Ordained May 7, 1844, he spent so much of his priest's life among Temiskaming Indians he wished to be buried among them in their Roman Catholic cemetery atop the cedar fringed sandhill overlooking the old Fort and Mission church. Camille Latour, James Kelly, Moïse Lavallée, James Quinn, Irenée Bellemare, Georges Cimogan and Salomon Massinikijik bear his pine casket up past the chapel shed where he first kneeled thirty-seven years ago. Up the pine needle pathway they climb to the small field of wooden crosses. Then, a week later they learn of Father Pian's August 1 death at Ottawa.

These deaths, though, little prepare Father Paradis for the crushing sense of September 14 loss when Bishop Lorrain transfers him south to Maniwaki Mission on the Gatineau River. As senior man in Temiskaming his nemesis, Father Nédelec, will stay on. Nevertheless, Father Paradis completes a seventy-two page description praising the fertile clay lands found on his latest trip north through Temiskaming. Decorating the text with water colour scenes and titling the manuscript a *Report* he presents it to Sir Hector Langevin, Minister of Public Works and leader of French Catholic interests in Macdonald's Conservative cabinet at Ottawa. Perhaps it may still help persuade the government to build a railway or a steamship way around or over the violent Long Sault obstacle to Lake Temiskaming. And complaining of Hudson's Bay Company's "heartless opposition", Paradis begs: Let the settlers in.

With barely enough time to pack personal belongings, Father Paradis must cancel his invitations for a previously arranged tour in September. Yet he argues its purpose was only to impress on Bishop Duhamel the successful but too slow progress of settlement in the two cantons along Temiskaming's eastern shore. No false flattery that one is named Duhamel, but could not the church more actively sponsor progress?

On October 26, Father Paradis is allowed to escort Augustin Laperrière, translator of the House of Commons; Father Thérien, chaplain of the Montreal Reform School and like Father Paradis, a tireless colonizer; Oliver Armstrong, chief immigration agent for the Canadian Pacific Railway; Joseph Larose, on his own way to view Temiskaming; and Messrs. Bouland and Meshine from Paris, France, scouting Canada for settlement opportunities. Cruising the burnished waters of Lake Temiskaming with Father Provost, the latest superior of Saint Claude Mission, aboard the *Mattawan*, they circle the upper lake and go ashore at Baie des Pères to ride horse drawn wagons along Alex Dupont's road east through Duhamel canton to the riverside farms of Francis Menard, Alfred Fournier and Thomas Larouche. Under a pale blue sky the last leaves of autumn glow orange against the background purple of spruce. Cows graze the stubbled fields, pigs wallow in barnyard sties. No time yet, though, for porches to front bare log homes.

After listening to first hand accounts of their delightful trip, Bishop Duhamel makes November plans for La Société de Colonisation du Lac Témiscamingue. Father Gendreau, Augustin Laperrière and Ottawa merchants P.H. Chabot and R. Ennis form the organization committee. Within two weeks the bishops of Ottawa and Pontiac declare their patronage of the new Society. December 12, the Society elects Father Gendreau as president, P.H. Chabot vice president and Augustin Laperrière one of the five directors. Their main aim? To colonize the north end of Lake Temiskaming, especially Duhamel and Guiges along with adjoining lands east where ground for another two cantons waits. Most importantly, the Society will offer assistance.

To make it easier for settlers to buy and occupy land, the Society, after promising to have Paul Dumais finish surveying Duhamel and Guiges, obtains permission from the Quebec government to act as real estate agent. So for a membership fee of $100.00, payable at $20.00 a year or more over five years, with the first year's payment made even more manageable at $5.00 every third month, more settlers will be able to afford a move to Lake Temiskaming. In return, the Society provides a lot of 100 acres with ten acres cleared, ready for cultivation, and pays Quebec the $30.00 purchase price. For now, though, the available land within Duhamel and Guiges limits the Society to 100 members.

Alex Lumsden, who has spent the summer building a depot camp at the head of the Long Sault, welcomes this colonization society. Owning 200 square miles of timber limits around Kipewa and Quinze lakes, he needs a steady supply of local hay and manpower for his shanties. Rinaldo McConnell, Jr., though, no longer cares as he has left this Ottawa River country to cruise the untouched timber stands around Sudbury station. And when he and Louis Riopelle take to prospecting instead the bush west of where Mattawa's Murray Syndicate bought mineral land last February, they too stake a claim on the southeast quarter of lot two, concession four of

Snider township. What the church colonization society is promoting in Quebec's Temiskaming region, maybe minerals will prompt in Ontario.

Lake Temiskaming Settlements - 1884 -

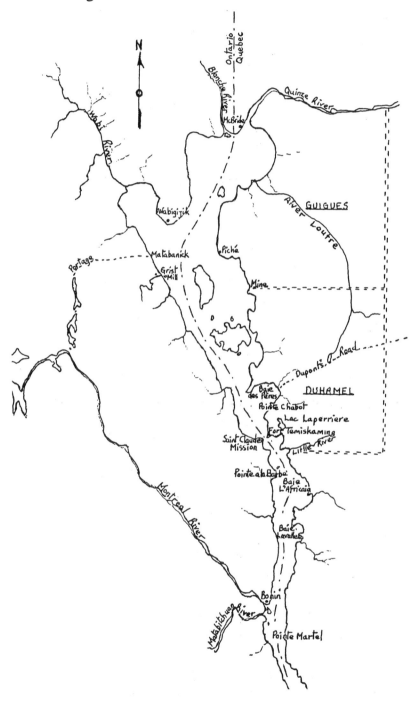

Yet in completing a fifteen mile bush road next year, 1885, between Mattawa and the foot of Seven League Lake, Ontario does show $15,000 worth of initiative. Furthermore, to persuade the Oblates that their colony is equally welcome on the west side of Lake Temiskaming, the Ontario government will soon survey an orderly township surrounding the Old Mission. And it will even honour this new township, as is the custom across the lake, with the name of another Oblate bishop, Lorrain.

Now with a road around the river's lower and middle rapids, Quebec and Ontario settlers may walk an easier way north to Captain Bergerons' little steamer which for a small fee will carry them on to the bottom end of the Long Sault and the overnight luxury of David Fleury's new hotel six miles away at the head. But to get there, for the inexperienced, the river portage north is still Mount Everest high.

Then the Oblate's Colonization Society has a better idea. If the Federal government will grant $3,200, Father Gendreau promises to build tramways around La Cave, les Érables, Montagne and Long Sault rapids. A more direct route this will be with assistance for the settler all along the way. Since its January 8 provincial patent denies the right to build a railway, the Society plans instead to have horse drawn tram cars ease the burden of carrying loads around impassable rapids. Too punishing long, though, is the Long Sault haul, even for horses. Hector Langevin quickly makes sure his Public Works office grants the tramway money but as a locomotive will be needed for the Long Sault run, the Society must apply to the coming October session of Parliament for an amendment to the existing January charter. And before application, the Society must prove the cost of a railway route. Without delay the Society has Paul Dumais leave his survey of Guiges township to explore the cheapest, most level six mile railway alongside the Long Sault. To clear the chosen route during the winter, Pierre Bouilliame will manage a hundred men.

Charles Smith sympathizes with the settlers' transportation plight. He has the latest contract for weekly mail service to Lake Temiskaming. Leaving Mattawa at 7:00 o'clock every Tuesday morning, he does not arrive at Opemican post office until Wednesday evening. Even though, his Snake Creek dogsled trail does avoid the six mile torment of Long Sault.

Last June, the Public Works Department of Ottawa did send engineer Thomas Guerin to determine the cost of Father Paradis' scheme to dam and flood the Ottawa River. Too expensive, he decided. Too quick a rejection, though? The planned drop in lake level would uncover much valuable Ontario and Quebec farmland at Temiskaming's north end, Father Paradis raises his exiled voice.

Unaware of this rancor, Georges Jodouin, one of the Colonization Society's first members to reach Lake Temiskaming, clambers over the side rail of the *Mattawan* into a small rowboat taking him and his family to the shore of Baie des Pères. From there they walk east six miles along Dupont's muddy Duhamel road past Fournier and Menard's farms to 100 acres in the seventh concession, with ten acres already cleared. And here a community grows.

Still, though, too slow and expensive a growth. And because of its distance across the lake, John Piché's grist mill on the creek near Louis Sirouin's Big Pine clearing is of no use. Cheaper it is for the farmers on the Quebec side to sell their excess grain to the shantymen and buy flour from the old Hudson's Bay store at the Narrows. Half a barrel costs $6.00. Lard costs 30 cents a pound, tea a dollar, a page of pins for the seamstress housewife another dollar. And these are just bare essentials.

Needing cash himself, one occasional customer at the store Louis Sirouin tells C.C. Farr he has several tons of hay for sale at his Matabanick acreage. Would Farr be interested in checking its quality? And he mentions it may be his last crop. When Farr does sail north in late July he lifts his canoe ashore on to the beach just south of the big pine and walks up the narrow length of corduroy road curving slightly northwest through tag alders and cedar into the neck of Louis' small balloon shaped clearing. Up at its far end, past a small log barn to the right beside which two rounded hay stacks tower, a weathered black log shack with single slope of roof slumps over a tree-shaded gully curving down from a background ridge covered in poplar, spruce and birch. C.C. Farr sees Sirouin elbows on patched knees, hands covering his face, sitting on a balm of gilead stump beside the gurgling stream. Trapped in the vice of hermit existence Louis pounds his forehead until Farr calms him with quiet suggestions to move away: go back south and touch the hands of your people again. The Company will buy your hay and I'll buy your land with enough money to make up for anything you have spent. Restored to some sense of tomorrow, Louis agrees to Farr's offer of $20.00 for the squatter's rights and the need to go back to the old Fort to sign a properly witnessed sales agreement. Come back to the Fort for a decent meal and friendly company. And Louis does.

C.C. Farr has finally made his own decision. First struck, when returning from the frigid imprisonment of his 1874 surveying job, by the extent of undeveloped farmland in this upper Lake Temiskaming region, then fascinated by its gentle grandeur and green leafed shores, so frequently publicized by Father Paradis, he has often thought of settling with his young family on a farm of his own. Convinced Hudson's Bay Company days on Lake Temiskaming must soon end, and trained at Haileybury Public School in England to the rudiments of self reliance and public duty, why not, he asks, promote my own settlement on the Ontario side of the lake? How often has he stepped off the Matabanick portage on to Humphrey's old depot clearing to have his breath swept away by mountainous clouds lifting hills and lakewater above! When the Nipissing and James Bay Railway passes here, others will share the thrill, and, fingering the deep soil, will come to stay. Too fantastic a dream? What the Colonization Society plans for the Baie des Pères area, why not here?

C.C. Farr can never forget that May afternoon eleven years ago when life flashed as smooth and clean as the paddle pulling him south towards a fur trading future. Sun speckled slivers of birch jabbed the wide western shoulder of Lake Temiskaming. Sap green light pulsed along the wine red flush of branches. And a tiny clearing gleamed straw yellow under the canopy of blue sky. That same clearing may now be his for life.

Advice For Settlers

PROVISIONS NECESSARY FOR A FAMILY OF FIVE SAY FOR ONE YEAR.

8 Barrels of flour, at $5.25 per barrel...............................	$42 00	
2 " pork, at $13.50 "	27 00	
80 Bushels of potatoes, at 50c. per bushel................	40 00	
30 Lbs. of tea, at 50c. per lb.	$15 00	
1 Barrel of herrings	6 00	
½ " salt	75	
Cost of provisions...		130 75

SEED.

20 Bushels of potatoes, at 50c. per bushel.....................	10 00	
3 " wheat, at $1.20 "	3 60	
10 " oats, at 50c. "	5 00	
Cost of seed		18 60

OTHER NECESSARIES.

1 Axe	1 50	
1 Grindstone	1 50	
1 Shovel	40	
100 lbs. Nails	3 00	
2 Hoes, at 70 cents each,..................	1 40	
3 Reaping-hooks, at 30 cents each	90	
1 Scythe	1 00	
1 Inch Auger	1 00	
1 Inch and a half Auger....................	1 50	
1 Hand Saw..........................	1 50	
2 Water Pails, at 30 cents each	60	
1 Window Sash and Glazing	2 00	
1 Bake-oven.....	1 00	
2 Pots at $1 each	2 00	
1 Kettle	1 00	
1 Fryingpan...........................	60	
1 Teapot	50	
6 Small tin vessels......................	40	
3 Large tin dishes, at 50 cents each..........	1 50	
6 Spoons	25	
6 Knives and Forks......................	1 00	
3 Pairs of blankets, at $5 per pair	15 00	
2 Rugs for Quilts, at 50 cents each...........	1 00	
2 Pairs of Sheets	2 00	
1 Smoothing Iron	50	
1 Pig	3 00	
Total................................		46 05
Add one Cow		40 00
Hay for do first year.................		12 00
		$247 40

A wealth of lake, Temiskaming is. And in so many ways, Edward Wright reminds himself. With George Goodwin's Ottawa money and that of G.T. Brophy, he is sinking his mine shaft on the boundary line of Duhamel and Guiges another fifty feet. Galena ore samples, from 1877, assayed eighteen to twenty-four ounces of silver to the ton of waste rock. Certainly enough of a return to justify the five ton stamp mill being built today next to the headframe. But, just as important, what other minerals may rest in the rocks protruding out of the bush around Lake Temiskaming?

BIBLIOGRAPHY

01. Anglicanus, Julius, *Missionary Bishops, A Plea for Indian and Immigrants,* Wilting and Williamson, Toronto, 1871

02. Awdry and Green, *By Lake and Forest*, Private printing, London, 1909

03. Burpee, Laurence, *Highways of the Fur Trade,* Royal Society of Canada, Copp Clark, Toronto, 1914

04. Caron, Abbé, *De Troyes' Expedition, 1686*, Beauceville, Quebec, 1918

05. Cassidy, George L., *Arrow North, the Story of Temiskaming,* Temiskaming Printing, New Liskeard, 1976

06. Chenier, Augustin, *Notes Historiques sur le Témiscamingue,* Ville Marie, 1937

07. Eccles, W.J., *France in America.* Fitzhenry and Whiteside, Toronto, 1976

08. Eccles, W.J., *The Ordeal of New France*, C.B.C. Publications Branch, Toronto, 1969

09. Farr, C.C., ed. Roach, T., *Tales of the Wild North-East,* Highway Book Shop, Cobalt, 1980.

10. Farr, C.C. *The Life of Charles Cobbold Farr*, private printing, 1967

11. Gerin-Lajoie, Albert, 'Fragment From a Journey', *The Beaver,* Winter, Hudson's Bay House, Winnipeg, 1969

12. Grant, George, *Picturesque Canada*, Art Publishing Company, Toronto, 1882

13. Hillis, James, 'Life in the Lumber Camp', *Ontario History,* Ontario Historical Society, Toronto, September, 1967

14. Jenness, Diamond, *Indians of Canada*, National Museum of Canada Bulletin 65, 1960

15. Kennedy, Clyde, *The Upper Canada Valley*, Renfrew County Council, Pembroke, 1970

16. Kirkwood and Murphy, *The Undeveloped Lands in Northern and Western Ontario*, Hunter,Rose & Company, Toronto, 1878.

17. Laflamme, Jean, 'Naissance de la traité des fourrures en Abitibi au Témiscamingue', *De l'Abitibi-Temiskaming,* College du Nord-Ouest, Rouyn, 1976

18. La Société de Colonisation du Lac Témiscamingue, *Colonisation du Lac Témiscamingue et du Kippewa*, Ministère de l'Agriculture du Canada, Ottawa, 1888

19. Lee-Whiting, Brenda, 'The Fortunes of a Trading Post: Fort William, Quebec 1823-1869', *Canadian Geographical Journal*, LXXVII, number 1, 1968

20. Logan, W.E., Canadian Geological Surveys, 1845, 1863-66

21. Lindsey, Charles, *An Investigation of the Unsettled Boundaries of Ontario*, Hunter,Rose & Company, Toronto, 1878

22. Lower, A.R.M., *Settlement and the Forest Frontier in Eastern Canada*, MacMillan, Toronto, 1936

23. MacKay, D., *The Honourable Company,* McClelland and Stewart, Toronto, 1949

24. Mitchell, Elaine A., *Fort Timiskaming And The Fur Trade,* University of Toronto Press, Toronto, 1977

25. Mitchell, Elaine A., 'Frederick House Massacre', *The Beaver,* Spring, Hudson's Bay House, Winnipeg, 1973

26. McLean, John, *Twenty-Five Years' Service in the Hudson's Bay Territory*, volume 1, Richard Bentley, London, 1849

27. Morel, Leo, *Mattawa, The Meeting of the Waters*, Société Historique de Mattawa Historical Society, Mattawa, 1980

28. Nantel, *Notre Nord-Ouest Provincial,Étude sur la vallée de l'Ottawa*, Senecal et Fils, Montreal, 1887

29. Newton-White, E., *Gillmor of Algoma*, Charters, Toronto, 1967

30. Nish, Cameron, *The French Regime*, Prentice-Hall of Canada, Scarborough, 1965

31. Ontario Minister of Education, *Annual Archeological Reports*, Warwick Bros.& Rutter, Toronto

32. Pain, S.A., *The Way North*, Ryerson Press, Toronto, 1964

33. Paradis, Father Charles, *From Temiskaming to Hudson's Bay*, Buffalo, 1888

34. Proulx, J.B., *Au Lac Abbitibi*, Cadieux and Derome, Montreal, 1885

35. Rich, E.E., *Moose Fort Journals, 1783-85*, The Hudson's Record Society, London, 1954

36. Rich, E.E., *The Fur Trade and the Northwest to 1857*, McClelland and Stewart, Toronto, 1967

37. Ryerson, Stanley, B., *The Founding of Canada*, Progress Books, Toronto, 1975

38. Schull, Joseph, *Ontario Since 1867*, McClelland and Stewart, Toronto, 1978

39. Shakanash, *Canoe Trip to Fort Temiscamingue in '79*, Highway Book Shop, Cobalt, 1971

40. Sowter, Edwin, *The Highway of the Ottawa*, Ontario Historical Society Reprint, Griffin and Richmond, Hamilton, 1915

41. Speck, Frank, 'Family Hunting Territories, Social Life, Myths and Folklore of the Temiskaming Algonquins', *Canadian Department of Mine, Memoir 70*, Ottawa, 1915

42. *Statutes, Documents and Papers Respecting the Northern and Western Boundaries of the Province of Ontario*, Hunter,Rose & Company, Toronto, 1878

43. Sulte, Benjamin, 'Etienne Brulé', *Royal Society of Canada*, section 1, 1907

44. Sulte, Benjamin, 'The Valley of the Ottawa in 1613', *Royal Society of Canada*, volume X11, 1915

45. *The Algoma District*, Ontario Crown Lands Report, Grip, Toronto, 1884

46. Thompson, George, S., *Up To Date or the Life of a Lumberman*, 1895

47. Tyrrell, J.B., *Journals of Samuel Hearne and Philip Turnor*, The Champlain Society, Toronto, 1934

48. Wallace, W. Stewart, *The Pedlars From Quebec*, Ryerson Press, Toronto, 1954

49. Williams, G., *Andrew Graham's Observations on Hudson's Bay, 1767-1791*, Hudson's Bay Record Society, London, 1969

50. Williams, G., *Hudson's Bay Miscellany*, Hudson's Bay Record Society, London, 1975

51. Wintemberg, W.J., 'Early Names of the Ottawa River', *Royal Society of Canada*, section 11, 1938

INDEX

Brophy, G.T., 120
Brown, Nicolas, 68
Bruce Mines, 100
Brulé, Etienne, 6, 8, 9
Brunswick Lake, 50, 51, 54
Bryson's Depot, 100
Bryson, George, 65
Bryson's Island, Lake Temiskaming, 95
Budge, George, 59, 60, 63
Burgoyne, General, 38
Burns, John, 89
Burns, William, 89, 95
Burwash, Adam, 101
Bytown and Prescott Railway, 80
Bytown settlement, 70

Cahiague, village, 8
Cahill, Brother, 102, 103
Callander Station, 111, 112
Camboose shanty, 71, 72
Cameron, Æneas, 45, 48, 49, 52, 54, 55, 63, 64
Cameron, Angus, 54, 58, 59, 60, 61, 62, 63, 64, 65, 66, 67, 68, 69, 70, 71, 73, 74, 76, 83
Cameron, Donald, 80
Cameron, Elizabeth (Eppie), 70, 77
Cameron, James, 68, 69, 70, 77, 78, 79, 80
Campion, Étienne, 47
Canada, 3, 4, 5, 8, 9, 12, 13, 14, 34, 38, 77, 84, 100
Canada East, 83
Canada West, 80, 83
Canadian Pacific Railway, 102, 105, 107, 109, 110, 111, 112, 115
Canadian Free Traders, 65, 66, 67, 74, 80, 87
Canadian militiamen, 1, 2, 11, 16, 17, 18, 19, 20, 21, 26, 28, 31, 32
Capascoos, 60
Cap Rouge, 3
Carignan-Salières regiment, 11
Cartier, Jacques, 2, 3, 21,
Cartier, Jacques, 68
"Castor Gras" fur, 11
Cataracoui River, 11
Caya, Onésime Salois, 94
Cayuga tribe, 5
Chabot, P.H., 115
Champlain: see de Champlain
Charles I, King of England, 12
Charles II, King of England, 12
Charlton Island, 54, 55

Charron, Hyacinthe, 93
Chaudière, 85
Chenal du Diable, Lake Temiskaming, 103
Chenier, André, 47, 50
Chevrettère, Pierre, 83
Chevrotière, Sergeant, 16
Chicoutimi, 113
Chief Island, Lake Temiskaming, 27, 106
Chisholm, Roderick, 51
China, 12
Church of England, 79, 97
Cimogan, George, 114
Clément, Father, 76
Clauston, W., 103
Clouston, Edward, 42
Cocking, Matthew, 36
Cognac, fur trader, 22, 23, 24, 25, 28
Colbert, Jean Baptiste, 11 12, 13, 15
Collingwood, Canada West, 83
Commissioner of Crown Lands of Canada, 107
Compagnie de la Colonie, 29
Compagnie des Habitants, 9
Compagnie du Nord, 1, 2, 15, 18, 19, 22, 24, 84
Company of Adventurers of England Trading Into Hudson's Bay, 12
Company of One Hundred Associates, 9
Company of the Farm, 13, 15
Company of the West, 11, 13, 29
Congé system, 15, 29
Constant, Isaac, 47, 52
Constitutional Act, 1791, 45
Coppermine River, 36
Corlaer (Schenectady) settlement, 28
Couchiching Falls, 79
Coureurs de bois, 11, 15, 27, 29
Coursolle, fur trader, 45
Cree tribe, 6, 11, 12, 15, 33, 35, 52
Cromalty, William, 103, 105
Crooked Rapids, 85
Cugnet,François-Étienne, 32
Cumberland House, 37, 91
Cummings, John, 100

Debigarre, Brother, 103
d'Écrévisse, Indian guide, 89
d'Iberville, Sieur, 16, 17, 18, 21, 24, 25, 29
Dallas, H.B.C. Governor Alexander, 86, 87
Dawson, M.P. Algoma, 111
de Bellefeuille, Father Louis-Charles, 67, 68, 69
de Boisclerc, Nicolas Lanoullier, 31

McConnor, fur trader, 100
McDonell, Allan, 64, 65, 67
McDonnell, Alex, 77
McDougall, Alex, 47, 48, 49, 50, 51, 52,
    54, 55, 57, 58, 60, 64
McDougall, John, 95
McGill, James, 38
McGillivray & Day, 74
McGillivray's,Thain & Company, 61, 64
McGillivray, William, 51, 54
McKay, Angus, 41, 42, 43, 44, 45
McKay, Donald, 41, 42, 43, 44, 45, 54, 55,
    57, 58, 60, 61, 78
McKay, James, 78
McKay, John 61, 63, 64
McKenzie, Hector, 77, 78, 79, 80, 82, 85,
    87, 88
McKim township, 110
McLaren's Bay, 85
McLaren, David, 100
McLean, Roche, 95
McMartin, John, 94, 95
McMurrich, W.B., 112
McNabb, John, 57, 58
McOuat, Walter, 111
McPherson, Andrew, 62, 65
McRae, John, 62
McTavish, Frobisher & Company, 49, 51
McTavish, John George, 54, 55, 65, 77
McTavish, Simon, 38, 51, 54, 55
Mediterranean Sea, 28
Meech, shantyman, 85
Menard, Francis, 115, 117
Metabetchouan River: see Matabitchuan
    River
Metis, 69
Mexico, 2
Michilimakinac trading post, 29, 35
Michipicoten Post, 51, 54
MicMac tribe, 2
Miles, Robert, 76
Miller, Abitibi clerk, 104
Minisinakwa River, 58
Miron, Alfred, 86
Miron, Joseph, 85, 92, 93, 94, 99, 107, 108
Mission Narrows, Lake Temiskaming, 88,
    89, 92, 93, 97, 100, 101, 103, 107,
    109, 118
Mississauga tribe, 8
Mississippi River, 12, 14
Mitchell, Andrew, 66
Mofette, Brother, 93, 97, 98, 101, 012,
    103, 108, 109

Mohawk tribe, 5, 6, 9, 10, 11, 28
Monsipy River, 13, 30
Montagne, 117
Montagnais tribe, 6, 10, 21, 39, 56
Mont Laurier, 108
Montreal, 1, 2, 8, 9, 11, 12, 20, 21, 29, 30, 33,
    34, 35, 37, 38, 39, 46, 48, 49, 52, 55, 57,
    60, 61, 63, 64, 65, 67, 69, 70, 78, 79, 81,
    82, 83, 87, 91, 92, 94, 109, 112, 115
Montreal-Abitibi canoe route, 43
Montreal merchants, 11, 12, 14, 15, 29, 31,
    112
Montreal-Quebec merchants, 29, 35
Montreal Reform School, 115
Montreal River, 20, 21, 30, 40, 41, 43, 44, 56,
    70, 73, 83, 84, 89, 102, 111, 112, 114
Montreal River Island, Lake Temiskaming,
    84, 95, 97
Montreal River Notch, 21
Montreal & St. Jérôme Railway, 108
Moore, David, 108
Moose Factory Island, 52, 61, 63, 65, 68, 69,
    70, 73, 76, 79, 82, 91, 100, 112, 113,
Moose Fort, 30, 35, 37, 39, 42, 47, 50, 51, 52,
    55, 57, 59, 61, 91
Moose Island, Lake Temiskaming, 106
Moose River, 52, 53, 54, 55, 60, 65, 73
Moreau, Father, 74
Morrison, John 100, 109
Mourier, Father, 86, 102, 103
Mountain Rapids, 85, 112,
Mount Royal, 3
Mulligan, Captain, 97, 102, 107, 109
Murphy, William, 110
Murray Brothers of Pembroke, 86
Murray Mining Syndicate, 115
Murray, Thomas, 89, 99, 110
Murray, William, 99,110

Napoléon, 59
Narrows: see Mission Narrows
Nédelec, Father, 91, 92, 93, 103, 107, 113,
    114
Nelson River, 15
Neutral tribe, 10
New Brunswick House, 50
New Brunswick, province, 91
New England, 28, 29, 33, 34, 80, 109
New Farm, Lake Temiskaming, 63, 64, 69, 82
New France, 2,9, 10, 11, 12, 20, 29, 31, 33,
    34, 35
New Hampshire, 80
New North West Company, 51